# Praise for *Two Weeks to a Breakthrough*

"*Two Weeks to a Breakthrough* is going to be the least expensive and arguably the most effective purchase you will make if you truly want to change the direction of your life. Packed with practical examples and clear ideas for action, Lisa Haneberg's book provides a proven pathway to help you shift your focus and allow yourself a new set of choices for your future. Whether you want to find catalysts to provoke needed change or develop momentum to carry you through to success, this book shows you how and provides examples to inspire your journey. If you truly want to produce a breakthrough in your life, follow the daily practices Lisa prescribes and stand well back—the eruption of creativity and inspiration will amaze you."

> —Adrian W. Savage, author,
> *Slow Leadership: Civilizing the Organization*

"If you're stuck and needing to move forward, *Two Weeks to a Breakthrough* is just what the doctor ordered to get you out of your rut. Buy the book, do the exercises, and you'll realize that by focusing on the right actions, the lessons found in this book, every day you'll be one step closer to being unstoppable. With Lisa Haneberg as your guide, anything is possible!"

> —Phil Gerbyshak, author, *10 Ways to Make It Great!*

"Engaging, relevant, life changing. Want to make positive changes in your world? Lisa has a strategy that will help you speed up the process and make it happen."

> —Craig Huggart, trainer, Bradley Arant Rose & White LLP

"If you are looking for 14 easy steps to improve your life, keep looking. If you are willing to do the hard work, Lisa Haneberg has a program for you. *Two Weeks to a Breakthrough* is well designed and developed to maximize its effectiveness. Tired of simplistic checklists that never lead to change? Invest in yourself; read and apply Lisa's new book."

—Roger Shank, CPA and controller, City Securities Corporation

"As someone who tends to lose interest quickly when adopting new techniques, many of the 'improvement' books I read are beyond my disciplinary aptitude to sustain. This book is different. The prescriptive nature of *Two Weeks to a Breakthrough*, coupled with its rapid results, have proven to be just the ticket to keep me on task and give me the quick wins I need to keep going. And best of all, this book is now a repeatable process in my personal toolbox."

—Dwayne Melancon, software industry executive;
author, GenuineCuriosity.com

"The best way for businesses to flourish is to have self-aware leaders who lead by example. *Two Weeks to a Breakthrough* will challenge and reward those leaders who are ready to dig deep and recognize their own growth opportunities in order to take their companies or organizations to places they've never gone before. This book will ensure amazing breakthroughs for those who are ready to take on these challenges. This is the must-have book of the year!"

—Jodee Bock, owner, Bock's Office Transformational Consulting;
author, *The 100% Factor: Living Your Capacity* and youalready-
knowthisstuff.blogspot.com.

"This fine, nourishing, nurturing book is worthy of the attention of anyone wanting to make improvement in health, wealth, creativity, or relationships. I read so many books of this genre and am always delighted to find one that is thoughtful and adds something new to the world. And I am always happy to find a book that lays out practical steps without being insulting. I will be recommending this one."

—Stephanie West Allen, principal, Allen&Nichols Productions, Inc.

"A simple, concise, and powerful set of practical advice to give you the right mindset and momentum toward your goals."

—Bhushan S. Jawle, manager, Barclays Services Japan Limited

"In *Two Weeks to a Breakthrough*, Lisa Haneberg will switch you on to the excitement of key word possibilties: abundance, catalyst, manifestation, evangelism. Regardless of where you are in your personal or professional life, Lisa will guide you in rethinking success-provoking key words. Follow her advice to relax and meditate as you read—your synapses will be sparking with ideas and insights. You will be emailing her requesting a pre-publication copy of her next book!"

—Marnie Sweet, M.A., C.T.A., luxury travel consultant

"Lisa's chapter on goal setting goes beyond the smart approach and brilliantly outlines steps for defining life-changing, breakthrough-level goals that aren't simply fantasy. This chapter alone is worth the investment! The structure of the book is fantastic. The combination of step-by-step instruction, Lisa's ebullient style, and the notes from her program participants (both good and bad) make the process seem possible for anyone. A very detailed roadmap to a breakthrough!"

—Michael A. DeWitt, technology and change
management consultant, eFunds Corporation

"Stuck? A positive direction for change is not always easy to create. Use *Two Weeks to a Breakthrough* to keep a constant positive discourse with yourself. You will find a breakthrough every two weeks!"

    —Thomas Cooper, U.K. business consultant,
      Carroll J. T. Corporation

"It's one thing to tell someone to 'go off and make a breakthrough.' It's quite another to tell them specifically how they might go about it. Lisa Haneberg does the latter, laying out a cogent, achievable action plan for getting what you want efficiently and reliably. She identifies things to do, things not to do, things that facilitate progress, and things that retard it. You may be a hard-core procrastinator, you may be very busy, or you may really value your time. Whatever the case, you will find wise advice and council herein."

    —Steven Weiss, president, Watermark Consulting Limited

"Lisa Haneberg takes us to the crossroads of coaching, self-help, and personal development. She brings into the equation knowledge from the 'new' sciences of complexity and chaos, but in a very direct, pleasant, and to-the-point style. She shares a very personal view of how to attain a breakthrough in two weeks. Above all, the real interest of the book is the very practical way it pushes us into action."

    —Emmanuel Cuny, coach and facilitator, Arbovista

"Are you ready to achieve your wildest dreams? Have you read other books but not put their wisdom into action? Do you feel like you should be achieving your goals but resist them because you don't know how to create the plan? Lisa Haneberg has assembled a structured way to transform your life. Follow the instructions in her book and see if you don't find yourself in a new world in 14 days."

    —Blake Ragsdell, change manager

JB JOSSEY-BASS

# Two Weeks to a Breakthrough

## How to Zoom Toward Your Goal in 14 Days or Less

Lisa Haneberg

John Wiley & Sons, Inc.

Published by Jossey-Bass
A Wiley Imprint
989 Market Street, San Francisco, CA 94103-1741    www.josseybass.com

Jossey-Bass books and products are available through most bookstores. To contact Jossey-Bass directly call our Customer Care Department within the U.S. at 800-956-7739, outside the U.S. at 317-572-3986, or fax 317-572-4002.

Jossey-Bass also publishes its books in a variety of electronic formats. Some content that appears in print may not be available in electronic books.

**Library of Congress Cataloging-in-Publication Data**

Haneberg, Lisa.
  Two weeks to a breakthrough : how to zoom toward your goal in 14 days or less / by Lisa Haneberg.
      p. cm.
  Includes bibliographical references and index.
  ISBN-13: 978-0-7879-8482-3 (cloth)
  1. Success in business. 2. Success. 3. Self-realization. I. Title.
  HF5386.H2453 2007
  650.1—dc22

                                                                2006032164

Printed in the United States of America
FIRST EDITION
HB Printing   10 9 8 7 6 5 4 3 2 1

# Contents

*To all the beloved guinea pigs who helped make the Two Weeks to a Breakthrough program great. Thanks for playing.*

# Introduction

A fine line separates a great life from one that is unsatisfying or filled with regret. Two variables determine which situation applies to you. The first is your mind-set. Are your thoughts and conversations in alignment with success and fulfillment? The second is your actions. Greatness is about showing up; successful people do what others put off or ignore. The program I present in this book is designed for those who are willing to play full out for at least fourteen days. It helps tune your mind and actions for breakthrough results.

Of the work I have done over the last ten years, nothing has been more interesting and rewarding than catalyzing breakthroughs. I love seeing the proverbial light bulb flicker on and then blaze with energy and excitement. I get immediate reinforcement, too. A breakthrough is an emotional change that shows up physically. You can see it! Eyes dance and gestures animate to the rhythm of mental wheels spinning. Breakthroughs change both actions and words. Here are a few real scenarios:

- Lou was not listening to a word Angela was saying. He couldn't, his mind was racing too fast. Something she said earlier had given him an idea. "Of course, it's so logical, why didn't I think of this earlier?" Bouncing from his chair, he thanked Angela and trotted off to think through the details. The meeting in five minutes would have to wait.

- Stephanie felt excited, scared, and passionate the moment she realized what she wanted to do with her life. The insights had been building in conversations over several days. Then it happened. The thoughts and ideas came together, leaving her feeling like she had reached a mountaintop. The week before she'd lacked ideas and felt stuck. Now full of passion and drive, she saw a compelling new possibility. "Can I do this?"

- A rush of anger, denial, and embarrassment washed over Jean. "How dare that woman stand up in the middle of the seminar and say that my head and heart were obviously not focused on the class?" But the woman was right, and as Jean stood there, after feeling vulnerable and exposed, she tapped into her desire to learn from the experience. Feeling thankful, powerful, and free, she watched the circle of seminar participants transform from empty nameless faces into partners. She was seeing them, and the day, through new eyes.

Lou, Stephanie, and Jean each experienced a small and wonderful breakthrough. Although their circumstances were different, each felt a thrust of progress and forward movement. These moments are special. As a coach, trainer, and friend, I get a huge thrill out of helping people succeed.

Creations occur in many ways. Sometimes a single ah-ha gives birth to the final design. In many cases, though, products and services evolve over time and through trial and error. The Two Weeks to a Breakthrough program has blossomed over time and with the help of many beloved guinea pigs. The seeds were planted more than ten years ago, but an important and pivotal moment came in 2003. A client asked me to train him and his small team of six managers and supervisors. The conversation went something like this:

Client: I'd like to continue to develop my management team. Will you put something together?

Lisa: What kind of training would you like?

Client: I am not sure, what would you recommend?

Lisa: What's your desired outcome? If the training is wildly successful, what will be different afterwards?

*Client:* I would like for each of them to get what they need to be more effective and feel jazzed about their work. The team is successful, and I want to help them get to the next level, individually and as a team.

*Lisa:* What if the desired outcome of the training is that they experience a breakthrough in results, as individuals and as a team?

*Client:* Yes! That's what I want.

Eureka! A breakthrough for me. At that moment, the notion of a program designed to facilitate breakthroughs vibrated along my bones and sent my brain into overdrive. I quickly got to work bringing together into one training program everything I had learned about catalyzing breakthroughs. What fun! The training consisted of weekly two-hour sessions over six weeks. Participants selected a project or goal on which to focus and seek a breakthrough. At the beginning of each session, they reported on the progress of their project and how the assignments from the previous week's session either helped or hindered their success. I shared one or two distinctions during the second half of each session and then made assignments to apply the concepts in service of their goals.

The results were mixed. Two of the managers made some progress, but nothing that would qualify as a breakthrough. Two of the managers made excellent progress and experienced small breakthroughs. Three of the managers experienced major breakthroughs. With one exception, the team as a whole made great progress. Why the differences? In a word, the answer is application. The managers who had disappointing results were the most reluctant to take the coaching and often did not complete their assignments between meetings. The middle group did some of the work and was somewhat coachable. The three managers who experienced major breakthroughs were both engaged in the program and coachable. They took the coaching and it worked.

My techniques produced varying results, too. I noticed that the participants experienced more breakthroughs when I gave them assignments daily instead of weekly. Those who did the assignments every day benefited the most. By the end of the program I shifted the focus to days instead of weeks. I still offer this program to corporate teams and many of the techniques and distinctions remain the same.

The progress people were making in just a few days amazed me so much that I began experimenting with a program that offered different assignments each day. Within a few iterations, the Two Weeks to a Breakthrough program was born. This book outlines the two-week program that has helped many people reenergize their lives and realize their goals. The beauty of this system is that the techniques are simple. The toughest part for many people is moving beyond fears and bad habits.

What's the big deal about breakthroughs? I can trace most of my greatest triumphs and memorable experiences to breakthroughs. One moment I feel stuck, and then I experience a breakthrough and I'm zooming. My fascination with breakthroughs began when I noticed that I could change my mind-set and my actions to produce more breakthroughs. Now, breakthrough generation is an important part of my work and helps my clients produce better results. Although I've designed Two Weeks to a Breakthrough as a two-week program, you can use the techniques for any length of time. You may experience a breakthrough in just a couple of days. The magic lies in both the nature of the techniques and their repeated application. This is an important point worth repeating: *The magic occurs when you employ the techniques repeatedly.* Please trust me on this and be open and coachable to this suggestion. The key to your success is getting started and staying in focused action. If you stick with the program and do the daily practice every day, you will make extraordinary progress toward fulfilling your goal and you will experience breakthroughs.

Do you have just one hour a day to devote to this program? Would you like to experience a breakthrough and begin zooming toward your goals? If so, follow the techniques and suggestions that I offer here. Give it fourteen days. Two Weeks to a Breakthrough uses both repetition and gradual introduction of new techniques to increase your ability to discover and manifest new possibilities, the raw materials for a breakthrough. Through a combination of step-by-step instructions, examples, exercises, and illustrations, it will help you create momentum toward your work and career goals. The straightforward structure can easily fit into your already busy day. After fourteen days, you will have a new set of techniques to plug and play whenever you need to improve project progress.

## What Is a Breakthrough?

Some people describe breakthroughs as scientific discoveries or efforts worthy of the Nobel Prize. Others believe they can have breakthroughs every day. I prefer a broad and permissive view of breakthroughs. To me, a breakthrough is

- A moment when someone receives an insight, ah-ha! idea, cognitive snap relative to the preceding time period—an epiphany.
- Better than normal progress by an individual or small group.
- A quantum change, or a leap forward in thinking, action, or results.
- A change, be it small or large, accompanied by an acceleration of progress or sudden insight (transformative rather than incremental).

You've heard of mind over matter, right? This distinction applies to the ways in which we think of and experience break-throughs. If you think of breakthroughs as rare, elusive, and unlikely, you lower your chances of experiencing one. If you define breakthroughs as small thrusts forward, your mind will be open and ready to experience them often. In *Archimedes' Bathtub*, David Perkins writes, "The breakthrough transforms one's mental or phys-ical world in a generative way." Breakthroughs are distinct from most continuous improvement efforts because they jump the tracks of sequential thinking to create a quantum change in results. Something exists that did not exist before. The next step is clear. You seize an opportunity. You jump onto a new path. Breakthroughs are important and valuable. They can propel results to new levels in ways that continuous improvement cannot. How? Figure 1 shows the difference between breakthroughs and continuous improvements.

At work, home, and play, both breakthroughs and continuous improvement efforts are important and valuable. Some goals and problems lend themselves to a continuous improvement approach. If you want something big to happen, though, go for it! Breakthroughs help you generate a new future and come to the rescue when you are stuck or stalled.

Not all breakthroughs are positive. Some come as a result of dissonance. For example, you may realize that your goal does not inspire you any longer or that it is not worth your continued focus. This is a breakthrough because it is better to recognize the problem and change your goal than to continue to dream and hope for something that is not a good fit for you. It is common for program participants to get bogged down by poor habits and assumptions. All of us are often our own worst enemies, and the only way to get beyond

### Figure 1. Tracking Breakthroughs.

self-sabotage is to acknowledge what's happening and blast past obstacles.

For example, one past participant—I'll call him Jim—stated at the beginning of the Two Weeks to a Breakthrough program that he struggled to finish projects. He was an excellent starter, but quickly got bored and disengaged. Sure enough, a few days into the program he started to disengage—even though intellectually he knew the techniques would be helpful to him. The focus of his assignments shifted to include overcoming his challenge with implementation. His first breakthrough was dissonance and his second breakthrough was his realization that he was not holding himself to a high enough standard and that this could change in an instant. Recommitting every day to completion helped Jim develop new skills and habits that will serve every aspect of his life.

## The Breakthrough Model

The Two Weeks to a Breakthrough program is based on the premise that you will produce more breakthroughs and better results when you are both focused and in action every day. Figure 2 illustrates four levels of effectiveness. The best position within the matrix is the top right, where high focus and high action meet.

Focus begins when you are crystal clear about your goal and desired outcomes. You achieve ongoing focus when you ensure that

**Figure 2. The Breakthrough Model.**

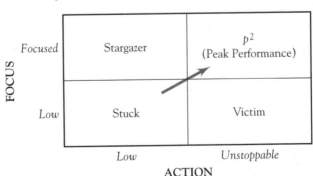

your goal stays top of mind and does not get crowded out by unrelated ideas, worries, or objectives. Daydreaming about goals can be a form of focus. So can talking to others about your goals. Learning can be a form of focus when it serves to clarify or define goals. The action component of the matrix measures activity level. Activity can include tasks, conversations (verbal or written), idea generation, problem solving, and learning that propels you toward your goal. Here is an explanation of each box in the model:

- Low Focus, Low Action: You are stuck, making no progress or even sliding backward. You are in a rut, feel uninspired, and may be apathetic. Others may see you as distracted, disengaged, or avoidant.

- High Focus, Low Action: You are a stargazer. Your days are filled with dreaming and great intentions with little or no execution. You might be described as all talk and no action.

- Low Focus, High Action: You feel like a victim, always moving fast but not going in the right direction. Low focus and high action often leads to excuses and victim conversations because you are working as hard as you can but not making progress. Others may see you as a whiner or complainer. Being a victim is tiring.

- High Focus, High Action: $P^2$—Peak Performance. You are really moving, positive both in speed and direction. You produce breakthroughs and feel satisfied. Your efforts are successful and your results are significant.

The Two Weeks to a Breakthrough program is designed to help you focus and become unstoppable. Each day you will work to crystallize your goal and take actions that can make a difference. If ever you feel dissatisfied with your results, look at the Breakthrough Model to determine whether your focus or action are lacking and in need of rejuvenation.

## A Review of the Two Weeks
## to a Breakthrough Program

The Two Weeks to a Breakthrough program includes some techniques that you repeat every day and others that you try on particular days. The suggestions fall into the following categories:

- The daily practice: Each day of the fourteen-day process, you will complete your daily practice, which is a combination of sharing your goal, taking action, and making requests. The daily practice changes throughout the program and serves to bolster both focus and action. Chapter Four, "The Big Power of Small Things," contains detailed information about the daily practice and dozens of examples.

- Focusing practices: On some days, you will perform tasks that improve your focus. Many program participants found the process of honing their goals extremely helpful. For more information about setting goals, see Chapter Three, "Setting Your Sights on Success."

- Action practices: On some days, you will perform tasks that increase the velocity of action in support of your goal. By the end of the book, you might be sick of reading about the power of small actions repeated again and again, but it's true! In fact, one of the most common reactions people have to the program is one of amazement that small actions can be so worthwhile. You will read more about this in Chapter One, "Manifesting Possibility," and Chapter Four, "The Big Power of Small Things."

- Obliterating resistance: Throughout the program, you will examine various sources of resistance and employ techniques that reduce or remove barriers to success. Chapter Two, "Breakthrough Catalysts," explores and illustrates the habits and beliefs that facilitate success.

In addition to your daily practice, each day has a theme. The theme serves to help you examine your goal from different angles and perspectives. Here are the themes for the entire program:

- Sunday, Day One. Launch: Wearing Your Goal and Defining Success
- Monday, Day Two. Conversations for the Change
- Tuesday, Day Three. Discovery
- Wednesday, Day Four. Connecting—The Share Blitz
- Thursday, Day Five. Fresh Eyes
- Friday, Day Six. What If?
- Saturday, Day Seven. Analysis
- Sunday, Day Eight. Wild Ideas
- Monday, Day Nine. Requests Blitz
- Tuesday, Day Ten. Playing and Planning
- Wednesday, Day Eleven. Action Blitz
- Thursday, Day Twelve. Giving Back
- Friday, Day Thirteen. Being It Today
- Saturday, Day Fourteen. Thanks and Reflection

## How to Begin the Program

I invite you to jump into your future with exuberance. Before you begin the Two Weeks to a Breakthrough program, read Chapter One through Chapter Four and complete the Priming the Pump exercise at the beginning of Chapter Five. Schedule time every day to do the exercises and your daily practice. Let your immediate family and coworkers know that you are embarking on a quest for multiple breakthroughs. Make sure you have a notebook or journal you can use to record your insights, setbacks, questions, and answers along the way. All these steps will improve your odds of success.

I would love to hear from you! I am thrilled to be guiding you through this program as your virtual coach and would love to hear about your experiences. You can e-mail me at lhaneberg@gmail.com. For more inspiration and to read about others' experiences with the program, check out my Two Weeks to a Breakthrough Blog at http://managementcraft.typepad.com/2weeks2abreakthrough/.

# 1

# MANIFESTING POSSIBILITY

In the universe of possibility, you set the context
and let life unfold.
> —*The Art of Possibility*, Rosamund Stone Zander
> and Benjamin Zander, p. 21.

Imagine going for a hike in the woods. No marked trails guide you, but you have a map, a compass, and a notion of where you want the hike to end. As you set out, you move to the left of that tree and to the right of the big one over there. Hopping over small streams, rocks, and tree trunks, you inch toward your final destination. With each step, you shape your direction and manifest possibility. As you move forward, some possibilities close out—but new ones emerge. Your compass allows you to navigate in broad swaths and keeps you from getting lost. Even with the compass, though, you cannot predict exactly where you will end.

Some decisions lead you into a section of the woods too thick with branches to be passable. You must backtrack to get moving forward again. Other fortuitous decisions make your journey easier or more interesting. You can see clearly a couple of hundred feet in front of you and try to strategize your moves to reach interim targets of trees, openings, and rocks. Looking at the sun's position and your compass confirms you are walking in the right direction. With every step you manifest one possibility and open yourself up to many more.

Take a hike! Exploring your life and work goals is much like the hypothetical hike that I described. You have navigational tools that are approximate and imperfect. Each decision and action nudges you forward and presents a unique set of possibilities that you can manifest. You can shape your experience and results through recognizing the myriad possibilities in play and making choices that seem directionally aligned with your goals. Each day you manifest possibilities—none purely right or wrong, but some will better serve your goals and catalyze breakthroughs.

A possibility is something that could exist, a potential alternative, a prospect, or a theory. Possibilities include potential outcomes, paths, flavors, efforts, paces, resources needed, experiences, and relationships:

- I will earn a Master's degree in the next two years.
- Bob's business will begin offering a new line of productivity products that launch in 2007.
- I can focus and be productive today.
- Sally will spend more time on high-impact projects and less time on routine tasks and meetings.
- The product development process will decrease to less than eighteen months.
- Maggie will fall in love and marry.
- The work environment will feel more invigorating and employee engagement will improve.
- Jack will shift from being a micromanager to one who empowers and engages his team.
- Art will partner with ten colleagues to create a project.
- We can achieve the goal with a $10,000 investment.
- Team members will build strong working relationships with one another.
- A new competitor will challenge your business.

These are all possibilities. At any given moment, including this instant, you have many possibilities that you can explore and manifest. You are probably unaware of most of these possibilities.

When you manifest a possibility, you reveal it and then make it real. To *manifest* means to make visible, and this can apply to tangible outcomes or intangible emotions and ideas. Here are a few descriptions of possibilities manifested:

- Harry was at peace for the first time in his life.
- As she collected her degree, she was flooded with emotion.
- Twelve months of hard work came together in victory as the new machine roared to life.
- Kelly was unable to outrun the police and was arrested for robbing the local mini-mart.
- Lisa's book achieved a top 10 ranking on Amazon.com on July 12th.
- Scott's e-mail, conversations, and tenacity paid off. After just two weeks he received fifty-five new orders.

Manifestations can be broad, large, narrow, or small. A friend of mine recently took over as president of a small company. At the time he accepted the job, many possibilities existed. He could play it small or lead full out. He could let his fears rule (this was a sizable promotion and he had doubts about his ability) or head into the role with a lion's confidence. The result? He has created a reality more powerful than he could have imagined. Not only is he an amazing president, he is perhaps one of the best in his industry. Possibilities existed that he could not see until he tuned his mind-set for greatness. But when he did—*pow*—magic!

Sometimes a country manifests a possibility. On September 12, 1962, President John F. Kennedy declared that the United States would land on the moon within ten years. Here's a quote from his speech:

> We choose to go to the moon. We choose to go to the moon in this decade and do the other things, not because they are easy, but because they are hard, because that goal will serve to organize and

measure the best of our energies and skills, because that challenge is one that we are willing to accept, one we are unwilling to postpone, and one which we intend to win, and the others, too.

It is for these reasons that I regard the decision last year to shift our efforts in space from low to high gear as among the most important decisions that will be made during my incumbency in the office of the Presidency.

Being the first to land on the moon was a possibility manifested by thousands of passionate and dedicated people. And at each step along the journey to the moon, project team members worked with determination and focus to make millions of individual decisions and actions come together for success.

The mountainous kingdom of Bhutan, sandwiched between India and Tibet, is one of the least economically developed countries in the world. Its average per capita annual income is about $700. Estimates of its per capita Gross Domestic Product (GDP), which have always been uncertain because the first modern census of Bhutan was not conducted until 2005, place Bhutan in the bottom 15 percent of countries. This is barely ahead of such impoverished nations as Djibouti, Rwanda, Burkina Faso, Tajikistan, Benin, Eritrea, and Mali. Living conditions in Bhutan can be harsh. Villages become isolated when roads are closed by landslides and less than two-thirds of the people in Bhutan have access to improved water supplies. Ninety percent survive by subsistence farming. The first modern roads were not built until the 1960s, and neither television nor the Internet were available until 1999. The Bhutan National Bank did not issue its first credit cards until 2004, and plans are only now being made to install the first automated teller machines in the country.

Despite its economic poverty and hardships, many people think of Bhutan as a peaceful Shangri-La that has managed to avoid the negative aspects of modern civilization. This is because of an intentional decision by King Jigme Singye Wangchuck to pursue a policy of increasing the Gross National Happiness rather than the Gross

National Product. First enunciated in 1972, when the king as-cended to the throne at age sixteen, the policy is based on promot-ing four areas of possibility: economic growth, cultural preservation, sustainable use of the environment, and good governance. The king's vision represented possibility on a grand scale. This was not the well-carved path that other countries hiked.

Scholarly research lends credence to the idea that happiness is not dependent on economic growth. In a paper published in the *Journal of Public Economics* in 2004, economists David Blanchflower and Andrew Oswald examined the degree of happiness in the United States and Great Britain during the 1970s, 1980s, and 1990s. Although some groups such as American men and African Ameri-cans reported increases in happiness, and people with high incomes and high levels of education reported more satisfaction than those with low incomes or the unemployed, the overall sense of happiness among Americans appears to have fallen over the years.

The people of Bhutan have manifested impressive possibilities. Life expectancy in Bhutan has increased and infant mortality has fallen under the policy of Gross National Happiness. Primary school enrollment has increased, with a goal of universal enrollment by 2007, and in recent years the government has spent as much as 15 percent of its budget on education. Economic growth has also been both strong and balanced by environmental preservation. Bhutan is developing hydropower resources while mandating that 60 per-cent of the country must remain forested. Twenty-six percent of the country is preserved as parks. The number of tourists allowed to enter Bhutan is limited to a few thousand per year and each tourist must spend a minimum of $200 per day. Hiking and trekking are encouraged, but high-altitude mountaineering expeditions were banned in 2003 in deference to spiritual beliefs. Bhutan became a tobacco-free country in 2005. Despite its successes, the coun-try continues to grapple with unavoidable outside influences in its attempt to balance happiness and economic growth. In response to concerns about the influence of television on young Bhutanese, the government recently banned both MTV and professional wrestling on television. Each year its leaders explore and manifest new possibilities that serve their goal of high Gross National Happiness.

The Bhutan example is evocative. To what degree do you measure success based on what you produce? If your ultimate goal is to feel fulfilled, connected, and joyous, your milestones ought not be about money, status, or possessions. What if you focused on manifesting possibilities that improve your individual, familial, or workplace happiness? When you shift your focus, different sets of choices emerge. This may not seem easy, and I struggle with it myself. As a recovering yuppie, my natural inclination is to define success by what I produce and the fruits of my productivity. Here's the catch and challenge: I know that I could work less and improve my happiness. Think about that. *I could work less and enjoy life more.* Seems like a no-brainer, doesn't it? That's what I thought, too, and I set out to change how I measure success. I have made great progress in the last couple of years and continue to manifest new possibilities for ways to increase my gross individual happiness.

What stops you from manifesting the life you seek? While you manifest possibilities every day, you may not be generating the reality that will best serve your goals. A barrier that affects many people is an unwillingness and inability to recognize the full range of possibilities. They give up too early or believe that because one option is no longer open, they can do nothing more to reach their goals. There are possibilities that you have not considered and that would allow you to spend more time on activities that enrich and enliven your life.

You can build your muscles for seeing, taking on, and manifesting possibilities by adopting the following states of mind: wonder, inquiry, abundance, exuberance, and courage.

## Wonder

When in a state of wonder, you feel admiration for beauty, welcome the unexpected and inexplicable, and are drawn to exploring the unfamiliar. You delight in pleasant surprise. Do you notice the extraordinary beauty all around you? Are you cognizant of your wonderful talents and gifts? Do the possibilities blow your mind and make you feel all tingly? For the next hour, try putting yourself in the mind-set of wonder. You will be looking at the world through a lens where anything is possible.

## Inquiry

When we see the wonders of the world, we seek to explore and understand them through inquiry. The art of inquiry is at the core of learning and great conversation. By asking provocative and evocative questions you will achieve many layers of understanding. When absorbed in inquiry, your mind's open-for-business sign is turned on and burns bright. Inquiry is how we interact with and relate to the world.

---

### Provo-Evo Communication

I have been using the term *Provo-Evo* in my coaching practice for some time. It's a combination of the terms provocative and evocative.

*Provocative:* Exciting and stimulating. Intriguing. What if . . . ? What's special? How'd they do that? Have you noticed . . . ? This team has the opportunity to impact the company's direction with its research. This problem has plagued the department for years—let's look at it from another angle. We need to come up with a short list of projects that will best support this goal, and all ideas will be considered. I'd like to pick your brain about a new idea I have been tossing around in my head.

*Evocative:* Pulls people in and helps bring things to mind. How did you do that? Tell me about your favorite. . . . If you could do it in any fashion, what would you do? Imagine the proposal is approved; what's our next move? You've come such a long way with this company and this year has been a great year for your project management leadership.

---

*continued*

Provo-evo is a way to approach inquiry and a tool for stimulating fresh thinking; yours and that of your employees, peers, and customers. It is a way of communicating that is engaging and connecting. If you want to experience many breakthroughs and improve your rate of success, master provo-evo communication. I think leaders ought to be master conversationalists. Your ability to provoke and evoke is an important aspect of conversation. I am an introvert, but I *love* a provo-evo conversation. This is an important point. Provo-evo transcends style and gregariousness. To be powerfully provo-evo, you must be sincere. The goal for creating great inquiry is not to see who can ask the most obtuse and intellectual question at the next staff meeting. It's about moving the conversation forward with velocity.

Are you provo-evo enough? Provo-evo inquiry unearths rich possibilities and paints a glow onto your goals. When you connect to others (provo) and they reflect because of your inquiry (evo), you tap into a deeper place in their hearts and minds, a place where the most interesting possibilities are kept.

## Abundance

To notice and manifest possibility, it helps to see the world as a place of abundance. The opposite of a scarcity mind-set, abundance is the belief that there is more than enough to go around. It's the belief that if someone else has launched the type of business that interests you, there is room for you both (or for hundreds of like businesses). It's the thinking that tells you there are many right ways to do things and if one approach did not work, many others have the potential to succeed. It's the mantra that competitors make excellent partners. Just because you are not first to market or don't have the biggest budget does not mean that you cannot be wildly successful. Abundance is the epitome of a win-win perspective. When you adopt a mind-set of abundance, you believe

- The market and potential are unlimited.
- The more I manifest, the more I can manifest.
- The resources and connections I need are available to me.
- The more I support others, the more resources I will have available to support others.
- If I seek input, I will receive generous wisdom.

Whatever your goal, you can find and use the resources you need to achieve success. Your success does not have to come at the expense of others. In fact, your success can support and facilitate other people's accomplishments. You can have your cake and eat it too. You can create a work life that is both prosperous and fulfilling. You can love your work and your life of leisure.

## Exuberance

*Exuberance* comes from the Latin *exuberare*, which means to be abundantly fruitful or fertile. A feeling of exuberance occurs when our minds are fertile and filled with liveliness, energy, and excitement. When exuberant, we grow luxuriantly. Exuberance is the inward personification of an abundance mind-set. While we each display exuberance differently (based on our unique personality and style), it's our state of being animated and vigorous.

Your physical energy impacts exuberance, but only a bit. The choice to be excited and engaged is mostly mental. Right now, as you read this, are you jazzed? When I schedule time to write, I go through a short psych-up routine where I turn my brain on the bright setting and get excited about the chapter or passage before me. You've likely heard about sports stars and actors who do this too. Your goal is important. Strike that. *Your goal is the essence of your life*. It is life. Exuberance offers possibilities that enable you to be amazing.

## Courage

Courage is another way of being that brings out your best. According to Gus Lee, author of *Courage: The Backbone of Leadership*, "Courage is a deep-seated, fundamental competence that leverages our other abilities. It invokes within us our absolute best selves. The tremendous results purchased by courageous behaviors can't be replaced" (p. 64). When we think and act with courage, we create a current reality and futures that could not have existed otherwise. Life changes for the better when courage walks into the room. Again from Lee's book: "Courage is manifested in courageous communication, courageous leadership, courageous problem-solving, and in resolving high-end conflicts" (p. 7). Courage is both a possibility and a catalyst. The courage mind-set helps you translate powerful possibilities into manifested greatness. Resolve, responsibility, and ownership are at the heart of our courageous minds.

Does reading about this collection of mind-sets make you sit a bit straighter in your chair? Are you thinking about your day in a new way? These heady concepts pack a punch and are not typical sources of conversation in many homes and workplaces. One of the unique aspects of the Two Weeks to a Breakthrough program is that these five powerful mind-sets form the program's foundation. While you are blazing through your practical to-do lists, you will also be seeing and manifesting new possibilities because your mind is being tuned for success.

I love this program because it allows me to work with and support many amazing people. The people I work with feel something big welling up inside their brains and guts. It's a deep desire to make something special happen. They want to manifest possibility and break through to immeasurable success.

# 2

# BREAKTHROUGH CATALYSTS

Your quest to manifest possibilities and generate breakthrough results will be easier if you identify and use catalysts. Strictly speaking, a catalyst is a substance that promotes a chemical reaction: it participates but is neither consumed by the reaction nor incorporated into its products. You have just as much catalyst at the end of the reaction as you did at the beginning. Catalysts will not cause reactions to occur, but they will help reactions that would have occurred without them proceed more quickly or at lower temperatures. In most cases the effect takes only small amounts of catalyst.

Catalysts work by providing easier ways for reactions to occur. In technical terms, they provide alternative reaction paths with lower activation energies. Every chemical reaction has a certain threshold, known as its *activation energy*, that must be exceeded for the reaction to occur. A catalyst does not lower the activation energy of the basic reaction; instead, it provides an alternative that produces the same results with a lower threshold. A good analogy is a bridge over a valley. Without the bridge, it might be possible to cross the valley by driving down one twisting road and then back up another. A bridge allows the valley to be crossed more quickly and with less energy. It would take as much energy as ever to drive down one side and up the other, but it's no longer necessary to do so because the bridge goes straight across to the same end point.

Another common example of a catalyst is the catalytic converter your car uses to help eliminate harmful carbon monoxide, unburned gasoline, and nitrogen oxides in its exhaust. Carbon monoxide is poisonous. Unburned gasoline reacts with nitrogen oxides to form low-altitude ozone, which is different from the beneficial high-altitude ozone that blocks UV rays. Instead, low-altitude ozone is a component of smog. Nitrogen oxides also contribute to acid rain and can irritate mucus membranes. Catalytic converters contain honeycomb structures composed of ceramics coated with small amounts of the metals platinum, palladium, and rhodium. Platinum and rhodium speed the conversion of nitrogen oxides into harmless nitrogen and oxygen, while platinum and palladium speed the conversion of carbon monoxide and unburned gasoline into less harmful carbon dioxide.

Many beliefs, actions, contexts, and habits have catalytic properties, too. Breakthrough catalysts facilitate faster or easier progress much the same way a bridge speeds your passage over a river valley. By providing alternative ways to manifest possibilities, catalysts speed the breakthrough explorer along. The actions and situations that catalyze one person's results may not similarly affect others. Breakthrough catalysts come in many forms and they will vary by individual. Even so, several types of catalysts work for many people: coaching, making unreasonable requests, meditation and relaxation, a change to an exotic context, the proverbial two-by-four, relentlessness, and evangelism.

## Coaching

I listed coaching first for a reason. At its core, all coaching should be catalytic. In fact, I believe that catalyzing success is the primary reason to seek or offer coaching. The coaching conversation is an exploration of how to help a client achieve personal goals and examine the forces aiding and hindering progress. The coach's questions and ideas become thought bridges.

I understand that not all coaching is catalytic. You have probably received coaching that failed to enhance your achievement or make your journey easier. A lot of what is called coaching is not; it amounts to little more than advice. Advice is rarely catalytic. Great coaching helps you learn about and adopt mind-sets that promote your discovery of possibilities (like those discussed in Chapter One).

That's my goal when coaching; to help my clients discover and then be ways that will best serve their success. It's a gentle nudge and occasionally a shove onto the right path. A catalytic adjustment that makes a big difference.

A coached nudge is precious and can set your mind aflutter with new and easier pathways to success. Many breakthroughs occur following Provo-Evo conversations with others. Catalytic coaching can come from a stranger on the bus or a best friend who has known you since you were both children. To experience more breakthroughs, seek and offer more coaching.

## Making Unreasonable Requests

Ask and ye shall receive, right? Making unreasonable requests is not as unreasonable as it may seem. I use the term *unreasonable* here to mean big. Unreasonable requests are big requests that most of us are generally too chicken to make. Chapter Four offers several examples and techniques for making unreasonable requests. Outrageous requests make great things happen. And talk about a bridge? A well-formulated request, when accepted by the person you ask, can reroute your progress and enable you to zoom to success. Unreasonable requests that are turned down can also serve as important catalysts because often a compromise solution is offered that is still higher than you would have expected. Making great requests is perhaps the easiest and fastest way to produce breakthroughs.

Mahatma Gandhi said, "If you don't ask, you don't get," and I believe this to be true. I have a weekly routine that has proven very successful. Each week I make several unreasonable requests designed to move various goals and projects forward. I have had some amazing things happen because of my requests. Most people want to help if they can and get a charge out of granting the request. Sometimes my requests are catalysts that enable the other person to experience a breakthrough! A granted request creates an immediate shift in circumstances and bolsters your goals and direction. Even if only one in ten unreasonable requests get granted, it will catalyze a new reality.

## Meditation and Relaxation

Meditation and relaxation practices promote clear thinking and reflection. Hectic schedules, endless meetings, and mile-long to-do lists clutter thoughts and block your creativity. When you relax your mind and body, you make room for new and different ideas. Some people use mental retreats to generate new ideas, refocus, and tap into their goals. Whether away, at home, or at the office, relaxation techniques are critical to your success.

Think about the bridge that spans the river valley again. Without the bridge, you would have to take a long and winding road down one side of the river, then cross the river and go back up the bank on the other side. You would encounter more potential hazards and burn much more fuel down there than you would up on the bridge. Now imagine that the river valley represents your busy day. All the distractions and competing demands act like the twists and turns of the road. Stress constitutes the force of gravity and the river's current you must fight to get across. Relaxation is the bridge. It clears your mind and offers simpler, more direct routes for your thoughts and ideas to travel. Ten minutes of meditation facilitates a relaxed state of focus.

Are you stuck in the office all day? Try urban mountaintop thinking. Find a peaceful corner or put on earphones during your break. Play music softly and be with your thoughts. Imagine you are sitting on a mountaintop gazing down at the valley or up into the fluffy clouds. When you relax, your mind and body should feel stimulated and more energetic. The positive circulation catalyzes your thinking and helps you shove aside competing thoughts or unrelated and unfinished tasks.

## Exotic Contexts

Something is *exotic* when it is out of the ordinary, striking, saturated with color, or foreign. Your context is your setting, surroundings, or circumstances. A change to an exotic context can serve as a powerful breakthrough catalyst. Imagine exploring a different culture, taking a new route home, or sitting in a meeting filled with people from another industry. Exotic contexts stimulate your thoughts and challenge your assumptions.

Contextual elements can be as broad as your country or time (think of the 1960s and the 1990s) and as narrow as your office furniture arrangement or mode of transportation. Work pace, policies, and general practices are part of the context. Shifting your context to something new, different, and even somewhat disturbing can provide a surge of learning and ideas. Try asking a different set of people to help brainstorm an idea or solutions to a problem. Asking different, perhaps even off-the-wall, questions will facilitate a contextual change and perhaps a breakthrough. To change your reality, change your context.

I enjoy Cirque du Soleil shows. They are inventive, imaginative, and stimulating. After one show, it occurred to me that this would be a perfect place to bring a senior management team the evening before an all-day strategy planning meeting. Talk about an exotic context and catalyst! If they went to the show in a state of wonder and inquiry, their strategy meeting—and the end result—would surely be very different.

## The Two-by-Four

It feels like you have been hit between the eyes with a two-by-four (piece of wood). When you deliver the two-by-four, you give direct, candid, and tough to hear feedback. For some people, the two-by-four is transformative and just what they need to get knocked onto the path of success. In *A Whack on the Side of the Head: How You Can Be More Creative*, author Roger von Oech writes: "We all need an occasional 'whack on the head' to shake us out of routine patterns, to force us to re-think our problems, and to stimulate us to ask the questions that may lead to other right answers" (p. 18).

My boss gave me the gift of a two-by-four about ten years ago. She informed me that I was very smart—but not much good as a collaborator, because I was acting too cocky and inflexible. The feedback was a precious gift. At the time, it felt lousy and my first inclination was to attack back. Fortunately, I thought about what she said and had to agree her feedback was spot on. My demeanor changed immediately and new possibilities emerged. Today's reality would look much different had I not received that benevolent whack between the eyes.

Highly sensitive or defensive individuals are less likely to respond constructively to strong and direct feedback that something they're doing is not appropriate. You might need to work a bit harder to present the input in a way they can hear it. If someone takes the time and demonstrates the courage to offer direct feedback, be sure to show your gratitude. It might not be easy to hear, but the two-by-four can jolt you on the right track if you take the information and use it to improve your results. Offered with good intent and care, the two-by-four can catalyze a breakthrough and help you launch forward. You can either be wrong and lost or insightfully wrong and found. Sometimes a breakthrough begins with alienation.

## Relentlessness

Getting into action is a great way to create momentum and put your goals and intentions into the world. Being relentless about activity has an additive effect that can catalyze major breakthroughs. Often thought of as a negative, relentlessness is the juice behind a "this shall be" attitude. When you resolve to make your goals happen and follow up on that determination with an unwavering dedication to taking focused action every day, you will succeed faster and better than you can imagine.

If you want to see relentlessness in action, read Scott's breakthrough journal toward the end of this book. Scott experienced many breakthroughs and succeeded in moving his goals forward because he was unstoppable. Every day, even while traveling, he did the assignments and then some. His commitment and action were unwavering and his results were excellent. Another benefit of Scott's relentlessness is that he inspired others around him. They didn't want to quit because they could see that he was not letting anything get in the way of his focused action.

What if, for the next fourteen days, you were relentless about taking on and conquering this breakthrough program? Think about a goal that is so dear to you that it deserves an unrelenting focus and implementation. Picture yourself as you cruise through the day. Now imagine what would need to change to jack up your focus and action. How does the relentlessness in your life look? Pick a goal and say, "This shall be."

## Evangelism

Evangelists are passionate, loyal, and dedicated. They are different from garden-variety fans. Someone who likes a product or company might tell a couple of people about a positive experience. Evangelists do that as the appetizer to a seven-course meal. An evangelist gets up on a rainy Saturday morning to hold picket signs for a favorite political candidate. One evangelist for blogger Guy Kawasaki spent hours of his own time creating a computer program that would help Kawasaki display blog readership. He did this on his own and without being asked! Evangelists become pace cars that spread positive news and engage new users. They are volunteer moderators on discussion boards and master connectors between companies and their users. If you research a problem using a search engine, chances are you will find the answer—and that it will have been posted by an evangelist.

Evangelists are fans jacked up on caffeine and they imbue the environment with love and fraternity. Evangelism is an excellent breakthrough catalyst because magical things happen when someone believes enough in you and your goal that they willingly advocate on your behalf. These inspired beings will enthuse you and others with their energy, loyalty, and passion.

One Two Weeks to a Breakthrough participant had a goal of implementing a new testing procedure within her quality control group. Her group consisted of professionals who test products, so changing the test methods and rationale was a big deal. Her big breakthrough came when a couple of her team members became evangelists for a new test process. They took on the cause as though it was their own and they infused the work environment with support and creativity. The evangelists put her goal on the fast track and helped it gain support from the other group members. If you want to implement a change, one of the most powerful ways to succeed is to enlist evangelists to adopt the change and run with it. You may lose some control, but the result is always better. Managerial control is way overrated and often gets in the way of breakthroughs.

You may have noticed a pattern in this list of breakthrough catalysts. Coaching is conversation pumped up to the max. Unreasonable requests are questions for the courageous. Meditation and relaxation help the mind and body go further and deeper. Exotic contexts are stimulating and provocative. The two-by-four effect is strong feedback. Relentlessness is drive in overdrive and evangelism is acceptance to the tenth power. Breakthrough catalysts are our everyday habits taken a level beyond what may seem normal or comfortable. They stretch you. To produce breakthroughs you need to play full out and be willing to extend yourself beyond what you have been doing.

Try this. Kick up the intensity of everything you do for an entire day. Sing in the shower. Combine your clothes in a new and funkier way. Take a different route to work. Say hello to people on the street. Share your thoughts more fully. Ask the big questions. Extend your walk. Ask your boss out for lunch. Arrive at meetings early and engage in lively conversation. Share your wildest ideas. Be out there. Be strong. Be bold. Set breakthrough catalysts in motion and let them do their work for you. Look out, the world is shifting on its axis!

# 3

# SETTING YOUR SIGHTS
# ON SUCCESS

I must tell you that I have mixed feelings about the value of goals. Goals are vital to success because they provide inspiration and a focus point. The formula for peak performance is a combination of high focus and unstoppable action. How can you make sure you focus in the right direction if you don't have goals that move and energize you? You can't. Creating and manifesting great goals fuels achievement and makes life fulfilling.

Goals are also the enemy. You cannot predict what is going to happen in the next year, two years, or five years. Even so, some people create goals with narrow pass/fail criteria. If they don't achieve exactly what they want (or think they want), they count that as a failure. Many people give up on goals because things don't go as planned. Here's a key point and important lesson: *Things don't go as planned.* Reality is always different from what we hope or imagine. If you perceive deviations as undesirable or as problems, then guess what? Your results will be disappointing. If, on the other hand, you see the twists and turns of life as part of the adventure, then you set yourself up to realize a future better than anything you could have planned.

Think back five years. What were your goals five years ago? What did you worry about most and did these worries materialize? What would you have imagined your job would be today? Would you have predicted the changes that occurred? If you are like most people, you could not have predicted today's life five years ago. What this means for goal setting is that it is more important to be jazzed about what you are doing and moving in a good direction than it is to have a detailed map of where you want to go.

Another problem I have with goals is that many people set goals that aren't inspiring or interesting (to them). Why would you do that? Why shoot for something that fails to stir your insides or make the hair on the back of your neck tingle? Most goals are simply not good enough for you and don't deserve your attention and passion. Before people begin the Two Weeks to a Breakthrough program, I help them clarify, shape, and define a proper goal. Much of the time participants start with something they call a goal that is either not really their goal or not crisp, clear, and inspiring. Goals are great. Goals are the enemy. Whether your goals help or hinder your success depends on their creation and application. I believe that goals are important tools to produce breakthroughs and they will also be a barrier to your success if not well defined and flexibly applied.

To get the maximum benefit from this program, select a goal that is inspiring and important to you. Be careful not to aim too narrow or too low. And, yes, it needs to be possible. I hesitate to write this because most people are too conservative when setting goals, so overly ambitious goals are rarely a problem. Goals are too high when you cannot achieve them with awesome focus and unstoppable action. If you're like most people, you won't even know what that looks like yet, so just forget that "need to be possible" sentence. Go for it! Here are several characteristics of great goals:

- Your goals should be meaningful and inspiring.
- Your goals should apply to *you*.
- Your goals should be something you really want.
- Your goals should be challenging—but achievable.
- Your goals should be simple to explain.
- Your goals should be measurable.

## Meaningful and Inspiring

This is not the time to wimp out or get conservative. Achieving a goal takes work, so it should be something that you can get excited about and that will make a big difference in your life. Your goals must be worthy of extraordinary effort. Goals are a compass—a guideline for decisions about how to live and grow. You don't want to use blasé goals at the foundation for how you structure and conduct your life.

You know a goal is inspiring when thinking about it makes you smile inside. I know when I've hit on the right goal because I will get a rush of emotion so strong my eyes tear up a bit. It's a *whoa!*-type experience. That's me, I'm an emotional girl. Hitting on the right goal might look and feel different to you. Whatever happens when you strike mental gold, that's what should happen when you define your goal.

## Apply to You

This is an important distinction. I once worked with a mother who wanted her son to get better grades. This was not a good goal because it was not clear who should be taking action. A better way to express this goal would be this: *I want to provide the coaching, support, and ideas that will help my son willingly do his best in school and achieve excellent grades.* Your goals need to relate to the possibilities you want to act on and manifest.

This distinction is often lost on the leaders I work with. I have coached many managers who had goals that started off something like this:

- Goal: Fewer errors and improved yield.
- Goal: I want my employees to be more engaged and committed to their work.
- Goal: Operate safely.

The first problem is that these goals are all as boring as the goal of flossing before you brush. The second is that it is not clear to whom these goals should belong. Who commits the errors? Who will improve yield? Who will need to change to make employees improve engagement? Who operates safely? If you are a leader, make sure that your goals express the contribution you will make to achieving the result. For example: I want to create an environment that enables my employees to focus on quality and includes the information and tools they need to produce an outstanding product. I will listen carefully and genuinely to my employees and use their recommendations to make the workplace look and feel better and more productive.

## Something You Want

You might argue that if your goal is inspiring enough, it should pass this test as well. Even so, I think the topic of *want* is important enough to address separately. Your goal should be something you want to achieve even if the work will be hard, uncomfortable, or require life changes. More money or further promotions are rarely compelling enough on their own. Most people want money and achievement but this kind of score-keeping rarely stokes anyone's fire. What drives you to be at your best? Focus on the work you love doing and tie that into your desire for prosperity and accomplishment.

I have worked with several people who started off with a goal that they did not want. Their goals were ones they thought they ought to have or that were suggested by bosses or spouses (redundant, I know). I can empathize with the need or desire to please or placate others, but your goal will become a hindrance if it does not speak to you and make you sing with joy. Your bosses may think otherwise, but they don't want you to focus time and energy on something that appeals to you less than prime rib satisfies a vegan (or a Tofurky satisfies a carnivore on Thanksgiving Day). Why? You will not operate at your animated best because you are parading around in the wrong skin. You are singing "Oklahoma!" in the musical *Grease*, putting on a Speedo to play tackle football. It's just not right, so don't do it. Generate goals that excite *you*. Sure, you need to keep the people you care about happy, too. Maybe that's the start of a great goal—to be so turned on and engaged with life that it enriches and improves the lives of those I care about. It's a start. . . .

If you should want to achieve your goal, it makes sense, then, that your goal should not be something you don't want. Goals that articulate what you don't want are counterproductive.

Lots of people want to lose weight, so let's apply this thinking to a goal about weight. If your goal were to lose fifty pounds and not be fat, your time and energy would be focused on what's wrong (you're fat) and the weight you don't want. In business we know that you produce results based on your focus and action. This works for personal goals, too. I think the weight loss industry has things backward. You want to feel great, be healthy, and look your best, right? If you think too much about not being fat and not being overweight, you will be sealing your fate to be fat and overweight. Think possibilities, not problems.

Goals about negative things that you want to stop are not inspiring and they focus your attention in the wrong place. If you want to stop blowing up at staff meetings, that's great and I would encourage you. You should not be blowing up anywhere. Your goal should articulate the kind of leader and partner you want to become.

## Challenging but Achievable

As I typed this heading, I hiccuped a bit. What I really think is that your goals can be crazy as all get out. Crazy, crazy, crazy. Zany, mad, off the wall and beyond comprehension. Play out there. Do you think Michael Jordan's goals were conservative? Would Oprah recommend playing it safe? Are the Google founders thinking small? No, of course not. That being the case, the proviso does not make sense. And yet it does.

I have worked with several people who created goals that were not big enough—and still unrealistic. For example, going from GED to Ph.D. in a year is unrealistic. It is also way too small for a goal, just not inspiring. Going from no business to comfortable retirement in one year is also unrealistic. (Unless Oprah features your product!) Unrealistic goals such as these would only hinder your progress. It is not helpful to create a goal that has a stated end that does not fit or is not possible. Instead of saying you want Bill Gates's job and bankroll by next spring, have the courage to articulate the amazing success you could create. Here's an example: I write business books, so saying that I wanted to be featured on the *Oprah Winfrey* show would be dumb. Oprah does not talk about business books. A better, and ironically bigger, goal would be that I want to write books that are insanely useful to millions of professionals. Setting the goal of writing something insanely useful applies much more to the work I have chosen. It also describes, in big terms, the contribution that I can make through my books.

I am suggesting that you play big, but make sure you are on the right playing field. For the Two Weeks to a Breakthrough program, you will define two goals: one long-range and the other the progress and breakthroughs you want to experience during the fourteen days of the program. This will be an interim goal that supports your larger, long-term goal. Both must be inspiring, about you, and realistic (in a very big way).

## Simple to Explain

You should be able to explain your goal in a sentence or two. What's your elevator speech? Can you explain your goal to a perfect stranger in one minute or less? In the first three or four days of the program, many participants experience breakthroughs when they share their goals with others. The first few attempts are rusty and uncomfortable. After a few tries, they find they settle on the words that zero in on what they want to say and resonate with their listeners. Try it—each time you hear yourself sharing your goal, your mind recommits to it. That's an added bonus.

Another thing that often happens is that when you start sharing your goal you realize that you don't know how to explain it. You don't know how to explain it because you have not really figured out what you want to do. This is an extremely valuable exercise! One of the best ways to hone and focus your goal is to share it. After you have done this for a few days, you will get to a crisp statement that you can share in a elevator ride or while standing in line for a latte. A well-defined goal goes *pop*, and you will notice that you light up when sharing it (if you don't, you aren't quite there yet).

## Measurable

You need to be able to measure your goal, but not with three-decimal-point-within-five-percent-error-margin accuracy. Your goal does not have to be something that you can attach exact numbers to; after all, life is not that precise. It is critical that you be able to define success. How will you know when your goal has been achieved or exceeded? What does success look like? You cannot determine the exact outcome, so it is best to define success in a way that allows for wonderful surprises and slight changes in direction.

Defining success is important. If you do not know what success looks and feels like, how will you make the best decisions about which possibilities to explore and manifest? Recall the walk in the woods from Chapter One. If you have no compass, how will you know that the left you just took around the pond is pushing you off track? How you define success becomes a filter for the daily decisions you make.

What's your goal? Describe it to a few friends or family members. Say it aloud to yourself five times. Is your goal clear and compelling? Are you tingling inside? Do your friends and family understand what you are trying to accomplish? If you are having a hard time explaining your goal, you probably don't have it adequately defined. Start by describing what success looks like. Be specific and determine how you will know when you have achieved your goal. Test your goal against these criteria and tweak it if necessary. Here are some samples of goals that are unhelpful and need to be clarified or redefined:

- I want to be making $100,000 a year by the age of thirty-five.
- I want to get promoted within six months.

- I want to graduate from college.
- I want to be a good manager.
- I want to complete the barge project on time and under budget.
- I want to launch a Web development business.
- I want to be more organized.

Conversely, I could get excited about these goals:

- I want to manage in such a way that I am able to create an environment where my employees can and want to do their best work. I want to be a positive role model and inspiration for excellence every day.
- I want to create an online marketing business that allows me to use my ever-growing knowledge and passion for the field and its technologies to help small business owners grow the businesses they love.

Zowie! Imagine sharing those goals with a perfect stranger while waiting in line to buy tickets to see *String Cheese Incident*. You will change that person forever—and yourself, too! I would like you to spend some time thinking about your goal and the short-term goal you want to create for this program.

1. What would a home run look like during this two-week program? How about a grand slam home run? What would make you say, "Wow, I made unimaginable progress toward my goal!"?
2. Break this interim goal into a goal for this week. What would a home run look like for this week? And what about today? To make the week's home run occur, what would a home run look like today?
3. What does long-term success look like? How will you know when you have arrived? How will you define success (remember Bhutan)?

I have to remind myself to do this all the time. If we can visualize achievement and mentally practice, it improves performance. Actors run through lines in their minds. Lawyers visualize their closing arguments. All of us do this all the time. Become one with your goal and resolve to make it so.

> When you visualize, then you materialize. I think
> if you've been there in the mind, you'll go there in
> the body.
> —*Denis Waitley, Ph.D., psychologist (from*
> *http://thesecret.tv/teachers.html)*

# 4

# THE BIG POWER
# OF SMALL THINGS

If you remember and apply just one concept from this book, I would want it to be this one. *Small actions can move mountains and shift realities*. Small actions applied consistently will do nothing less than change the world. Small becomes big.

As a trainer and executive coach, I have seen thousands of tiny acts make big differences. It's exciting to observe. The question that turns the meeting on its end. The sudden inspiration to visit a museum that leads to a career change. The phone calls you make day after day and that finally pay off big. The new method that becomes your signature. Sometimes the impact is immediate, like when a blogger posts about a favorite new gadget and sales go through the roof in under an hour. Sometimes the big effects are delayed, like when you rediscover your youthful ambitions by leafing through an old photo album.

Often, small actions start a chain reaction of other actions that build and develop until—*pow*—something happens. A job opening is posted at your company. It's not exactly a match to your past experience, but you find it highly appealing. You decide not to apply. You mention the job to your wife at dinner. She picks up in the tone of your voice that you want to apply and encourages you. You don't apply. The next day, you go for a walk during lunch and see street performers. You decide to apply for the promotion. You don't get the job. The news is tough to take because you had already mentally moved out of your current job. It's no longer interesting or challenging. Over the next few months, you go to more association functions and talk to people differently from the way you did before.

Prior to the job posting, you went to these functions and acted like a smug jerk (you weren't looking for a job). But now you want to learn about what's going on and whether the grass might actually be greener somewhere else. You click with a couple of people. You exchange cards and a few e-mails. You have coffee with a like-minded colleague who works right around the corner from your office. She just heard ABC is launching a new division. She can tell that your interest is piqued and suggests you call ABC and ask for information. You put off making the call. You mention the ABC project to your wife and she can see in your eyes you want to call. She encourages you to call. You don't call. You read an article about Richard Branson's new spaceport venture in New Mexico. Your boss does something stupid at work. You make a call and talk to the expansion leader at ABC. As it turns out, you met him at an association function a couple of months ago and sat at the same table for dinner. Luckily for you, this occurred after you stopped being a smug jerk at these meetings. You have coffee with him the next day and—*pow*— your career takes a new and exciting direction. Tiny snowflakes together create an avalanche of change. If any one action had not occurred, the outcome would have been very different.

This idea that small changes can make a big difference is nothing new to those who follow chaos theory. The *butterfly effect* is a widely popularized interpretation of one of the key elements of chaos theory. Simply put, the idea is that something as seemingly insignificant as a butterfly flapping its wings in the rainforests of Brazil has the potential to trigger a tornado in Texas. The flapping wings stir the air and the effect grows into a meteorological event of epic proportions. If the butterfly hadn't flapped its wings, the tornado wouldn't have occurred. If the butterfly had flown in a different direction or been in Tahiti instead of Brazil, maybe the result would have been a typhoon in the South Pacific or a hailstorm in Russia instead of a tornado in Texas.

The butterfly effect has its roots in something that mathematicians refer to as *extreme sensitivity to initial conditions*. That means that even small and seemingly insignificant changes at the start of a process described by certain kinds of equations can produce wildly different and practically unpredictable results. During the early 1960s, when American meteorologist Edward Lorenz was developing some of the first computer simulations of weather, one day he wanted to repeat the last steps of a previous simulation. Because computers of the time were slow and difficult to use, he tried to save some time by using the intermediate output from a previous simulation as input for a new simulation. Doing so would save him the trouble of repeating calculations that weren't of interest while still giving him the results he needed. Or so Lorenz thought. To his surprise, the results of his second simulation were much different from the results of his first simulation even though they should have been virtually identical. Lorenz eventually discovered the source of the difference: the simulation program internally calculated results to six decimal places but rounded them to three decimal places for output, and he used the rounded output as input for the second simulation. That small difference in starting values produced two completely different sets of results. Mathematicians had long known about sensitivity to initial conditions, but Lorenz's work emphasized how important they can be in real-world applications.

Although Lorenz originally quoted a colleague who had made reference to the flapping of seagull wings, he eventually switched to butterflies and used the title "Predictability: Does the Flap of a Butterfly's Wings in Brazil Set Off a Tornado in Texas?" for a presentation at the 1972 meeting of the American Association for the Advancement of Science. The practical implication is not literally that a butterfly can cause a tornado half a world away, but rather that sensitivity to initial conditions makes long-term weather forecasting a practical impossibility.

Lorenz eventually simplified his model and reduced the number of equations from twelve to three. He discovered that in addition to its sensitivity to initial conditions, for certain input values the system would change over time but repeatedly return to certain states or combinations of variables he called *attractors*. Scientists and mathematicians working on chaos theory have since discovered many other kinds of attractors, but the particular set discovered by Lorenz continue to bear his name and are often used as a classic example of deterministic chaos.

Figure 3 shows the result of calculations based on the same three equations used by Lorenz, with the black and white balls representing two sets of initial conditions that differ by only 0.001 percent. The paths traced by the balls in three-dimensional space represent the evolution of the system over time. At first, the paths defined by both kinds of balls are virtually identical, but as time passes the paths diverge and the sequence of results defined by the black balls becomes completely different from that defined by the white balls. Regardless of the initial position, the state of the system will circle around one attractor and then the other, but the sequence of events is different for each possible starting point.

Chaos theory is cool. We can see a sensitivity to initial conditions in many aspects of our lives. Small changes in new employee orientation reduce turnover. Good running shoes reduce injuries and could improve the overall health of someone fifteen years later. A new job is posted. Little things can make a big difference.

Three beliefs will help you put the big power of small actions to work in creating breakthroughs and generating a life you love. The first is that you are not in control. You need to let go of any need to know which action, or combination of actions, is going to make things happen. In chaotic systems, and your life is a chaotic system, you are not in control. Some actions will impact the system and others won't seem to make any difference at all. They may become important at a later time or never.

Instead of trying to control what you cannot, focus on putting lots of directionally aligned actions out into the world. This is where the power of small actions repeatedly applied comes into play. You don't want to waste time with actions that do not line up with your goals. Focus is always important. If you can take a few small and aligned actions every day, you will experience breakthroughs and produce great results.

The second belief I recommend is that you will be more successful if you act from a position of sincerity, passion, service orientation,

# Figure 3. Lorenz's Attractors.

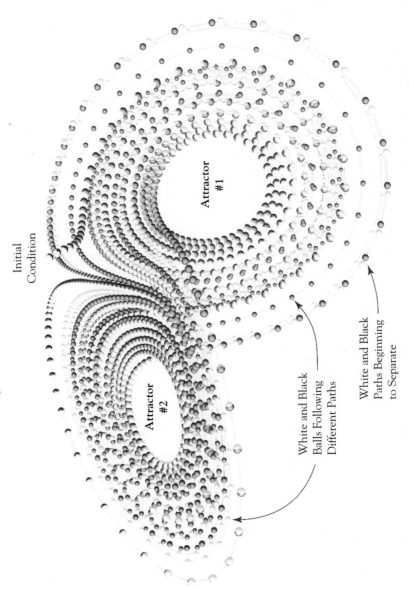

Initial
Condition

Attractor
#1

Attractor
#2

White and Black
Balls Following
Different Paths

White and Black
Paths Beginning
to Separate

and gratitude. The magical and mystical powers of small actions will flourish more when people sense that you are working on something larger than yourself. If you believe that you are somehow entitled to a breakthrough or due for one, this will come through in your actions and dull their effect. This belief gets to the question of why you do what you do. What's driving you to succeed? If you need to see a tangible result from every action you take, you are measuring success in a way that will hinder your success.

The third belief that will serve you is that life is about the journey and not about the goal. Ten years from now, you will recall and tell stories about your experiences along the way, not the end result. Goals and aspirations provide some focus for how to live today, and you need focus to feel great about where you are heading. Where you end up is not nearly as important as how you get there. Pour your energy and focus into today's journey. If you do this, your tomorrow will be much better. When you adopt this belief, you will increase the power and appeal of your little actions. Small deeds can be done today. They exist in the present.

Flap your butterfly wings. Flap, flap, flap. Each small action is another flap. You never know the impact each tiny flap might have. Today's flap might catalyze tomorrow's blizzard of changes. You never know what's possible!

## The Daily Practice

The daily practice is your tool for capitalizing on the big power of small things. Without exception—I mean that, *without exception*—past participants of the Two Weeks to a Breakthrough program have said that the daily practice was the key to the program. Everyone agrees that the power of the program lies in providing a structure that ensures they stay in focused action. Small actions make a big difference.

The daily practice is both the most important and dreaded element of the Two Weeks to a Breakthrough program. You might find it intimidating at first, but I promise that it will get easier each day.

During the program, I ask that you complete the daily practice every day, including the weekends. Here are the components of the daily practice:

- Tell people about your goal.
- Take actions that support your goal.
- Make requests that support your goal.

When I first created the program, the daily practice was the same every day—tell two people about your goal, make two requests, and take two actions. Over the last year I have changed the daily practice to reflect how human goals develop. At the beginning of the program the emphasis is on sharing your goal. Toward the middle of the two weeks, the emphasis shifts to making requests, and the later days stress actions. The daily practice for the two-week program looks like this:

| Day | Daily Practice |
| --- | --- |
| 1 | Three shares and three actions |
| 2 | Three shares and three actions |
| 3 | Three shares and three actions |
| 4 | Share blitz—lots of shares |
| 5 | One share, two requests, and three actions |
| 6 | One share, two requests, and three actions |
| 7 | Three short actions (weekend pace) |
| 8 | Three short actions (weekend pace) |
| 9 | Requests blitz—ten requests |
| 10 | One share, one request, and four actions |
| 11 | Action blitz—ten actions |
| 12 | One share, one request, and two actions |
| 13 | One share, one request, and two actions |
| 14 | One share, one request, and two actions |

You can do the daily practice in person, by e-mail, phone, blog, or other means. It is important to mix things up a bit and involve new people each day. Telling the same four people about your goal for two weeks will help a tiny bit; sharing with different people each day will pay off big. Feel free to combine shares, actions, and requests to maximize your time and results. For example, you can tell someone about your goal and then make a request. One clarification: although telling someone about your goal and making a request are technically actions, my intent is that you complete other actions each day. Actions can be small, like signing up for a newsletter, registering a business license, or asking three people for ideas at lunch. Periodically complete larger tasks like creating a business plan.

Please trust me when I say that the daily practice is the key to generating breakthroughs. The key. Doing the daily practice facilitates focused action and it is the constant rhythm and momentum that is magical and life giving to your goal. Even if you never do the two-week program, adopt the daily practice. It's that powerful in a delightfully simple way. I love it that the key to breakthroughs is so basic and easy to do! Here are a few comments about the daily practice from past program participants:

> I'm having a good experience with the Daily Practice. As I've mentioned on the blog, I am not naturally inclined to talk up my business with other people. I've started just by contacting people in my immediate network—other developers I work with, previous work acquaintances, etc. I have two lunch meetings now scheduled for next week.

> My favorite, or in my opinion the most effective part of the program is the daily practice. It's pretty amazing how two small actions, letting two people know and two requests can make a huge difference in achieving my goals.

> I have been continuing my practice. It's great. I put faith in the process and it's working. In fact, I will be continuing to use this process in the future many times. It's that good.

The daily practice is my savior. :-) I have a tendency to overanalyze things. I always procrastinate by reading more and more information and end up in paralysis by analysis. By making sure I'm doing the daily practice, I'm forcing myself to move forward. The fact that I only need to do two things helps a lot, since in the past, I got overwhelmed by the complexity of reaching my goals because I look far ahead.

Thanks Lisa—if it wasn't for this program and the daily practice, I might not have picked up the phone to make that call. I am really glad I did.

This Two Weeks to a Breakthrough program really rocks—the value of daily practice implemented passionately is proving to be a wonderful investment.

The daily practice is hard! I think about it a lot but I have discovered that making requests is the hardest part. I haven't had much trouble sharing my goals with two people each day and I haven't had any problem taking some sort of action each day. But the request part has been hard.

I had a breakthrough of massive proportions—directly as a result of being committed to doing my daily practice.

This has been an awesome experience for me. The breakthrough was beyond anything I even dared to dream—and all because of the daily practice. I know my product/service is good, but it was only through implementing the daily practice, that others were able to appreciate it as well.

There were elements of the daily practice which tested my resolve and that I would rather have sidestepped (requests and sharing). However, the structure of the program and the "nudges" kept me on track and I found that as soon as I did the parts that I would rather have not done they were not so bad after all. And they did yield results! I have a whole list of un-requested requests that I can return to in the next week or so too and it's become a habit that whenever I'm meeting or on the phone with a colleague that I will also mention my goal and ask them what they think etc.

The point of the daily practice is to help you create a presence, platform, and place for your goal and to make new things happen. Doing your daily practice every day will help you achieve your goals. Start the daily practice today! Here are a few techniques for the elements of the daily practice: sharing your goal, making requests, and taking action.

## Sharing Your Goal

When I talk to people before they begin the Two Weeks to a Breakthrough program, I often hear resistance in their voice when I discuss the importance of sharing their goals. I think we hesitate to share our goals because we know that once we out ourselves, we need to take responsibility to own our goals. Yes! When we share goals, we are also saying them to ourselves and reinforcing what matters most. If you share your goal enough, you will wear down your internal resistance. It's powerful. Actions that are inconsistent with your goals stick out like Shaquille O'Neal at a conference for steeplechase jockeys.

In addition to tuning your focus and reinvigorating your commitment, sharing your goals also serves an important purpose related to the butterfly effect. When other people know what you are up to, they make things happen. Small things that make a big difference. They might offer their help or make a helpful suggestion. People become connectors hooking you up with people you ought to know. They remember your goals and talk about them at art shows and dinner parties. Like birds that spread and fertilize seeds, people help one another's ideas and endeavors grow. Every time you share your goal with another person, you hand out seeds to spread on your behalf. People love to be connectors!

When you share your goal, do so with exuberance. Show your passion and don't be afraid to express what's important to you. In Chapter Three, I offered a couple of examples of compelling goals. Remember this one?

I want to create an online marketing business that allows me to use my ever-growing knowledge and passion for the field and its technologies to help small business owners grow the businesses they love.

Use this structure and create an elevator speech that explains your goal. You might want to add a question to the end: "I'd love to pick your brain for input on my business model. Can I buy you coffee next week?" Test it to make sure that you are not wimping out. If you said, "I want to create an online marketing business" and stopped there, you would be wimping out. Don't wimp out. The big power of small things beckons you to be authentic, real, and energized.

## Making Requests

The types of requests that I find make the biggest difference are not necessarily the "give me" kind, although sometimes you should ask for something you need. Most of the time, you will be requesting someone's time, ideas, connections, counsel, mentoring, projects, accommodations, or participation. Here are a few examples of these requests:

- Time: I am working on a project and would like to bounce a few ideas off you. May I buy you coffee one day this week so that we can chat (or may I ask for thirty minutes of your time over the phone)?
- Ideas or information: I want to help improve the workplace and would like your ideas. I'm inviting a few people for a brown bag lunch brainstorming session. Can you attend?
- Connections: I would like to build my online business. Can you suggest a few people I should get to know in this field?
- Counsel and mentoring: You are one of the best in your field. Would you be willing to mentor me? Perhaps we could start with a thirty-minute phone conversation or chat over coffee?
- Projects: I want to develop my skills in this area and would like to participate on the XYZ project because I think it

would help me and I could contribute to the group's success. I would be willing to lead the group if that's preferable. Can you help me get on this project?

- Accommodations: I am working on a goal that is important to me and that will make a big difference. Over the next month, I would like to change my schedule slightly so the project will fit in. I have worked it out so this change does not affect my other projects. Can I get your approval to _____?

- Participation: I am working on a book called _____. I have attached the book proposal for your review. I have great respect for your work and would love to have you write the foreword.

The best requests are win-win. I have created new jobs for myself several times—and my employers accepted the ideas because I was able to explain how the changes would benefit the company. Requests are powerful and few people make enough of them. Two Weeks to a Breakthrough program participants often have trouble coming up with requests. But once they get started, their creative floodgates open and they never look back. A great example of this can be found in Scott's Breakthrough Journal toward the end of the book. Scott became a master of making requests and they paid off for him.

A request is a question. Questions elicit responses. Are you afraid of making requests because you might not like the answer? Do you feel uncomfortable responding to rejection? How you respond to yes, no, and maybe is important. Try this:

| | |
|---|---|
| *Request:* | . . . can I buy you coffee and pick your brain? |
| *Their response:* | Yes. |
| *Your response:* | Fabulous, thanks so much. What day and time works best for you? |
| *Request:* | . . . can I buy you coffee and pick your brain? |

*Their response:*   No, I am sorry I don't have the time.

*Your response:*   No problem, thanks for considering. Is there a book or trade magazine that you would recommend I read to learn more about the field?

*Their response:*   Sure, pick up . . .

*Your response:*   Fabulous, thanks so much. I will check it out.

*Request:*   . . . can I buy you coffee and pick your brain?

*Their response:*   No, but I am speaking at the university next week if you want to check me out there.

*Your response:*   Really, that sounds perfect. How can I register?

Yes, no, and maybe are all good responses to requests. The better you respond to rejection, the more those rejections will morph into different possibilities! If your request is accepted, show genuine appreciation and excitement. This will make people feel great about helping you. If someone does not accept your request, do not be disappointed and do not make them feel guilty. This is what keeps us from making future requests. Instead, thank the person for the consideration and, if appropriate, ask for an alternative suggestion. Your demeanor should be matter-of-fact and open.

Requests are not always successful. In fact, you should expect most requests to be rejected. On the occasions where they are accepted, requests make a big difference. Don't hesitate to e-mail questions to your favorite authors or business leaders. Attend author readings in your area. Attend free webinars in the area of your interest. Get out there and get to know the people who can help you move your goal forward.

When I make big requests, I will often start with the following sentence: "Feel free to say no to this request. It's no problem at all; I know you are very busy. That said, I would be thrilled if you said yes." I mean every word of this. I do not expect people to agree to my requests but they often do. I flap, they flap, and next thing you know, the forecast has changed.

## Taking Action

When you take action, you move your goal forward. It might be just a tiny hop, but it is moving. Action after action, the pace picks up—and before you know it, you are zooming with progress. Throw in a few breakthroughs that thrust you forward, and you will be reaching new heights of success. It all starts with just a few small actions every day.

Actions are the most straightforward part of the daily practice. Even so, many Two Weeks to a Breakthrough participants have remarked that they had previously underestimated the power of doing a little bit each day. Even fifteen or thirty focused minutes each day can make a significant impact. In addition to the tangible result of completing a task, staying in action also helps you stay focused on and connected to your goal.

If you do a little each day, you will never feel as though you have failed yourself. This is a common problem. Many people have told me that it is difficult to get going again after they have ignored their goals for a while. Guilt and destructive self-talk swirls downward in a vicious cycle. After a while, it seems like it might be too late to get going again. No! First, it is never too late to reengage with your goals. The possibilities might be different, but they exist. Second, if you do a little each day, you can get rolling again smoothly and quickly.

The daily practice can take as little as thirty minutes a day, or you might choose to spend a couple of hours. Some people do less on the weekends and others find it best to establish and stick with a routine. It makes no difference. Do the daily practice every day and in the way that works best for you. Just do it. It's Popeye's spinach for breakthrough achievement.

# 5

# THE TWO-WEEK PROGRAM

Ready to dive into the program? Fabulous! Let's get this achievement party started. You have embarked on a wonderful journey. Equate this to eating your oatmeal every day, doing yoga in the evening, and jogging six times a week. You are taking care of yourself and ensuring that you do whatever it takes to make your dreams come true and contribute your gifts to this world. I applaud you. Most people are not so engaged in life.

## Before You Begin

Many program participants have told me the Priming the Pump exercise was very helpful. It gives you a list of possible actions, shares, and requests to draw from throughout the program. Some days you will not need to refer to the list, but other days it will come in handy. By priming the pump, you make your creative juices flow and you create a defense mechanism against fatigue, procrastination, and fear. You might have a few mornings when you say to yourself, "I don't even know where to begin, so I'll deal with this later." Later never comes. If you have primed the pump, you can quickly look at the list for some small action that you can do without having to think much. This practice will keep you in action and focused.

Take some time to fill out this exercise fully. Ask your buddies to help you brainstorm if needed. Several program participants reported that they wished they had taken more time on the exercise. Some ran out of ideas, others found they needed to go back and think about each section again. You can download a free copy of this exercise from my website, www.lisahaneberg.com.

## Priming the Pump

Before Day One of the program, your job is to hone your goal and prime the pump for your daily practices. Some people find it difficult to come up with new ideas each day for the daily practice. This exercise will help you generate lots of ideas from which to draw during the program.

### For Sharing Your Goal:

List family members with whom you can share your goal. (Note—you can share your goal in person, over the phone, or via e-mail.)

List friends with whom you can share your goal.

List professional acquaintances with whom you can share your goal. Include colleagues, peers, managers, employees, and those who are a member of professional organizations.

List professionals you may not know but who would be good people to talk to about your goal. If you can't think of at least ten names, ask your professional acquaintances for the names of people they would recommend you contact.

### For Taking Action:

Actions can be tiny or huge. Mix it up a bit and make sure that you have fun while moving forward.

First, list appointments you should make with people to discuss your goal. E-mailing someone to suggest having coffee together is an action. Treating someone to coffee is another action!

List contextual actions you can take. What can you do to ensure your environment is supporting your goal? You might need to organize, try out a new tool or process, get supplies, or create a particular mood.

List the research you should do to support your goal. What books should you read? Which topics do you need to research? What training courses would help you reach your goal? Do you need to complete a business plan or obtain a business license? Do you need to learn a new skill? Do you need to develop your platform or improve your exposure? Do you need to adopt new habits? Do you need to understand the market or business trends?

List the planning needed to reach your goal. Are there materials to create? Plans to define? Milestones to execute? List the steps you know you need to take. This list will get much longer and more focused once you begin sharing your goal and making requests.

## For Making Requests:

Many people have a hard time making requests. I encourage you to get over this! You can start small if you like, but don't stay small. List requests you can make for these kinds of things:

- Appointments
- Feedback—picking someone's brain
- Reviewing materials
- Endorsement or use of someone else's materials, processes, or systems
- Training courses
- Using time more effectively
- Asking someone to do something for you
- Subcontracting pieces of work (like someone to redesign your Web site)
- Asking someone to be your mentor or coach
- Partnering with others

- Starting something
- Stopping something
- Volunteering your services
- Asking for business, a decision, or approval
- Sharing your work with others
- Resources needed
- Other requests

Once you have completed this exercise, you are ready to begin the program. Return to your pump-priming list every couple of days to add and subtract ideas as you hone your goal and focus. If you keep the list full of options, it will be much easier for you to stay in action during the fourteen days and beyond. Give this part of the program your time and care and you will get started with a robust road map for focused action and greater confidence.

## Getting Started

You will notice that I have started the program on a Sunday. If you work a traditional Monday-Friday schedule, I recommend beginning on Sunday because it will allow you to plan and be ready for action on Monday. If you work another schedule, or no schedule, you can adjust the program start day to suit your needs. The program runs for fourteen days straight including weekends. All work and no play makes us dull boys and girls, you say? No worries. You will notice the themes and daily practices for the weekend days are shorter and more reflective.

For each day, you will complete your daily practice and consider the theme for the day. The daily practice is what's most important. If you are grooving along and making good progress, you do not need to spend a lot of time considering the daily theme. Use the daily theme when you need it or have the time to explore it along with your daily practice. I have found that each person needs different catalysts and coaching to stay on track with the program. The daily themes are my way of giving you virtual coaching. I offer a distinction or pose a series of questions for you to explore. At the end of each day's description, I offer three challenges that will help you make the most of the daily theme. Past program participants loved the variety of the daily themes.

## Sunday, Day One: Launch—Wearing Your Goal and Defining Success

Yippee! Ready, set, go! Today's daily practice is three shares and three actions. Congratulations on your commitment to yourself. Today your job is to work on your elevator speech. An elevator speech is a quick—sixty-second—description of your goal and why it is important to you. Create a rough draft of your elevator speech. Check to ensure that it is clear, compelling, personal, challenging, and invigorating. Refer to Chapter Three if you need help defining your goal.

Share your elevator speech with as many people as possible, but at least three. Ask them if the goal is clear and inspiring, and whether they get the sense you are passionate about its achievement. After each practice share, make adjustments and try again. By the end of Day One, you should have shared your goal with several people and feel great about your tweaked elevator speech.

Do not underestimate the power of sharing! Amazing things happen when other people know what you are working on. They sense your interest and passion and create connections and opportunities that you would not have known about had you not shared your goal.

The second part of your daily practice is three actions. Take three small actions today. Send a few e-mails, read a chapter, and review your goals for the program (from Chapter Three). Become one with your goal and resolve to make it so. Celebrate that you have started the program. Get a fancy coffee and daydream about the journey. How will you fit this into your busy schedule? What can you do to make sure you make the most of this opportunity? As you sip your double tall latte, relish the power of playing big and being engaged.

---

### You can't give yourself a great scalp massage!

When you go for a haircut, have you noticed how great it feels when the shampooer gives your scalp a massage? It feels electric and stimulating. You tingle all over. Have you also noticed that it is impossible for you to do this for yourself and feel the same way? Keep your mind out of the gutter and stick with me. I am not a biochemist, but it seems to me that a few things are missing from a do-it-yourself scalp massage:

1. Surprise: There's no element of surprise, the massage recipient always knows what's coming.
2. Energy: It's just the person's own energy completing the electrical circuit. No new energy is added.
3. Attention: Nobody else cares; it's just not the same. Who wouldn't want a scalp massage from someone else?

A shampooer who massages your scalp is adding new energy, surprise, and stimulation. What's the point? The daily practice is designed to promote external massage and stimulation related to your goal. You can't possibly create the same effect or feeling yourself.

Your partner rubs your tired shoulders—feels great!

You rub your tired shoulders—does not feel great. No one can do it alone.

There's something stimulating and exceptional that happens when you invite others to hear and comment on your goals. Here's the moral of this story: Do the daily practice every day and stick with it. Get your brain massaged every day!

---

Your three daily challenges:

- What can I do to master my elevator speech?
- What can I do to get comfortable with sharing my goal?
- What existing forum or communication channel can I use to communicate my goal?

Flap, flap, flap.
From past program participants . . .

It was a terrific Day One for me. Despite being in meetings all day (and I do mean all day), I managed to get two of our directors on board with my goal, and have my boss's buy-in for holding a monthly "Best of the Biz" meeting to have postmortems of what we did right that month, with representatives from each department. My plan is to use that meeting as a tool to foster more positive communication across departments.

Day One was challenging and successful. The questions that you asked me were very helpful in reflecting on the day and creating greater focus. I noticed that a fair amount of negative self-talk crept in and I also noticed where I initially chose to put my attention. In an interaction with someone, I was given a lot of positive feedback and yet I chose to pay attention to the one comment that I perceived as questioning my value. Craziness! This was great noticing and I was able to turn it around somewhat.

I used Day One as a springboard for the rest of the two weeks. I don't have a fixed timetable but I'm working out the list of actions I need to take, and by focusing on a couple per day, I've found that it really takes very little effort.

About the first day: I basically combined the telling and requesting parts by asking three people to give me 30 minutes: five minutes to listen to my goal of starting a translation business; 10 minutes for them to ask me any question about my presentation; and 15 minutes for feedback, advice, and any other people they know that might be interested in hearing me out or helping me. I was surprised at how easy that went, in spite of my fears. Two of the people are friends and one is a casual acquaintance. Everybody was very helpful and I got about two dozen names and a ton of ideas.

## Monday, Day Two: Conversations for the Change

> The size of success is limited only by the size of your thinking. Thinking big begins with believing big.
> —From "The Magic of Thinking Big,"
> by David Schwartz (audio)

Welcome to Day Two! Today's daily practice is three shares and three actions. Continue to share your elevator speech and take a few small actions in support of your goal.

Let's explore how to make changes become reality. I have written that it is important to communicate your goal and allow others to enroll in it, so they want to support your efforts. For change to become reality, you should increase the number and quality of conversations in support of your goal. What people talk about makes a difference. Some conversations are helpful and others are not. Better conversations lead to more breakthroughs. I am using the word conversations broadly here—to include phone calls, in-person dialogue, e-mail, letters, journaling, nonverbal expression, and self-talk. For example, say you have goals like these:

> *Goal:* Improve your team's skills and ongoing development.
>
> *Helpful:* "I'd love to get your feedback on a few ideas I have for how to better develop team member skills. . . ."
>
> *Helpful:* "I have put together a plan and would like to share it with you. . . ."

> *Helpful:* "What do you feel you need to learn to be successful?"
>
> *Not helpful:* "Darn, another day that I did not work on the plan. . . ."
>
> *Not helpful:* "This company is going to continue to lose people the way things are going."
>
> *Goal:* Complete a gripping and well-written novel.
>
> *Helpful:* "Let's make a deal. Can we get up early and do the weeding and then I want to lock myself in my office and write from 10 A.M. to 1 P.M. . . ."
>
> *Helpful:* "I would like to find or start a critique group in my area, do you know of any?"
>
> *Helpful:* "I am going to write a chapter this week. If I send it to you on Saturday, would you mind looking it over?"
>
> *Not helpful:* "Darn, another day that I did not write."
>
> *Not helpful:* "I'm not feeling inspired right now. I can't write."

A couple of smart colleagues, Laurie and Jeffrey Ford, shared this helpful distinction in a training class years ago. Conversations come in two types—on the court and in the stands. Think of a college basketball game. The players are on the court and the spectators in the stands. The conversations that the basketball players are having on the court are much different from those the spectators are having in the stands. On-court conversations are aimed at making a difference. They are active. When we speak on the court we are players. Example: "I have noticed that we are losing some great people. I'd like to put together a plan for improving the environment and development so we retain our great people and attract the best folks available. Will you participate in a brainstorming session tomorrow?"

In-stands conversations are like water-cooler conversations. They are directed outward. Example: "Until this company changes its ways and stops treating people like disposable resources, it will continue to lose great folks." If you want to make something happen, you need to get on the court. Conversations in the stands make no positive difference and may make the situation worse.

How does this relate to your goal? Check to make sure that you are on the court with your goal. Get on the court and have helpful conversations. Notice your conversations today. Notice the difference in what follows on-court and in-stands conversations and how they make people feel.

One last thing for today: Refer to the Breakthrough Model in the Introduction (two-by-two matrix of focus and action). Are you stuck, playing a victim, a stargazer, or heading into peak performance? Do something today that moves you in the right direction (toward the top right corner). Are you engaged and committed to your goal? Check your mind-set and self-talk. Acknowledge the barriers that seem to be getting in the way. Create and complete one action that helps remove a barrier. Create a list of three people you don't know, but should. Contact them.

How many people have you shared your goal with? Make today the day to spread the word in many channels:

- Fellow workers-managers, peers, or employees
- Loved ones
- Friends
- Your network, e-mail lists, casual acquaintances, blog, and so on
- Strangers (people you don't know but should)

Your three daily challenges:

- What can I do to engage in helpful conversations?
- What can I do to remain on the court?
- What can I do in the first half of the day to demonstrate focus and unstoppable action?

Flap, flap, flap.

From past program participants . . .

An interesting ah-ha came from looking at the focus/action matrix: I noticed that I have stargazer tendencies. I think the approach of picking specific, deliberate actions each day will make a big difference in the progress toward my goal.

The focus/action matrix also really helps me. I liked what Lisa said, "When you are not moving towards your goal, you have to either increase your focus and/or actions." That way, I immediately know what the problems are whenever I'm not moving.

Yep, just on Day One and Two, I'm excited about actually doing something instead of just thinking about all the projects that could be done but am too lazy to do.

I think I am unfortunately in the stuck mode on the breakthrough matrix. I have lots of ideas but I can't honestly say that I am focused. Moving to stargazer would be an improvement! But I'm pushing myself to take action at least. I only made one request today but it turned out to be a great one with a positive response so I'm building the muscle.

## Tuesday, Day Three: Discovery

Man cannot discover new oceans unless he has the courage to lose sight of the shore.

—*Andre Gide (French writer, humanist, and moralist, 1947 Nobel prize for literature)*

When we seek to discover the best in others, we somehow bring out the best in ourselves.

—*William Arthur Ward (American scholar, author, editor, pastor, and teacher)*

After all these years, I am still involved in the process of self-discovery. It's better to explore life and make mistakes than to play it safe. Mistakes are part of the dues one pays for a full life.

—*Sophia Loren (Italian film actress)*

> The real voyage of discovery consists not in seeking
> new landscapes but in having new eyes.
> —*Marcel Proust (French author)*

I love that last quote . . . *having new eyes.* This is something I have applied (and need to continue to reapply) with regard to my health. My new eyes? Creating health and longevity as a value and passion. I have some fixing and correcting to do before I can claim real health, but my habits and self-talk are fighting me less than they have in the past. New eyes. . . .

Today's daily practice is three shares and three actions. Continue to share your goal and take small actions that support your goal. The theme for day three is discovery. You have spent the last couple days refining your goal, sharing it with people, and taking action. Take a few moments today to ask and answer these discovery questions:

1. Who are the keepers of the current wisdom in the area of your goal?

2. Notice the parts of the program that are easy or difficult for you. What observations can you make about your areas of resistance?

3. What should you explore today?

4. Who are you being? What mind-set and self-talk are you operating under?

Thinking about that fourth question—here are a few ways of being that could pose a challenge for you (although they can be helpful in some situations):

*"I don't know anything and am unworthy."* This may come up when it is time to make requests, and you think, "Who am I to ask this person to help me?" If you feel this way sometimes, adopt another and more powerful belief. You are a professional with a great idea, goal, and mission and it is a privilege for people to help or mentor you. Most people enjoy helping others.

"*I know.*" Some people are a bit cocky. This is not a bad thing—indeed, it's a strength in many situations. When it comes to creating a breakthrough, however, it is best to be confident, open, curious, and *humble.* If someone you contact offers an idea or tells a story about something they have tried, be thankful, gracious, and resist the need to tell your own story or say, "I know."

"*I am getting ready.*" This belief is also known as paralysis by planning. Some folks spend most of their time getting ready to act. They create to-do lists, buy books, take seminars, and create multiple plans. All these are helpful and needed, but they must not get in the way of moving forward. At some point, planning needs to give way to doing! People who struggle with paralysis by planning are also often stuck in the stargazer quadrant of the Breakthrough Model.

Perhaps you are a better starter than implementer (this is a common complaint I hear). I can relate to this. Here's a technique that I have found helpful for becoming a better implementer and finisher. People often value ideas and define success in terms of having great ideas and getting things started. Try changing your definition of success. For example, here are two ways to define success:

- I want to generate great ideas and get my projects approved.
- I want to be known for generating great ideas and for my ability to put those ideas into practice. I am successful when I can see my work fully implemented.

Just about everyone has many more ideas than they can possibly put in place. Try defining your success in terms of projects and end products you deliver to your company or clients.

Discovery. Out there. And inside. Enjoy a few contemplative moments today. Put on your favorite thinking music and take thirty minutes to relax and let your mind wander. Be in the moment and enjoy the space you are in. It is wonderful to be engaged and active, isn't it? I feel honored to be a part of your journey. I hope that you are finding the program helpful so far.

Your three daily challenges:

- How can I get linked into and get to know the keepers of wisdom?
- How will I put myself into the mind-set that is open and ready to discover?
- What can I do today that would facilitate self-discovery and reflection?

Flap, flap, flap.
From past program participants . . .

I realized that the ideas I have, and carry around with me, when communicated to the world can return their worth tenfold.

"I'm getting ready" describes me well. Of course, for writing a book, I think a plan is good. But I also spend a lot of time reading about writing. Not as helpful. I'm definitely a Stargazer. Today, though, I broke out and wrote about 300 words. That's pretty good considering I had to take my girlfriend to a retirement banquet, and then we're going out with some friends after that. With my efforts last week, and my drive this week, it seems that the writing is coming a lot easier. I wrote the 300 words fairly quickly. No more waiting for inspiration to come, I am creating it now.

"I'm getting ready" resonates with me as well. I'm a strong planner, and even enjoy the process at times. Unfortunately, I get way too wrapped up in it, and it replaces execution.

## Wednesday, Day Four: Connecting–The Share Blitz

Today's daily practice is shares, shares, and more shares. If you're sticking with the plan, I applaud you! Most people in this world are not so engaged in creating an exciting new future. Your project may be large or small, but the act of getting active and focused and being passionate about your outcome makes you special.

A coaching client asked me what sort of people I prefer to work with. She was thinking about levels, like senior management versus middle management versus individual contributors. I was quick to respond, because this is an easy question for me to answer. I most like working with people who are up to something and want to make things happen. Level, function, or industry makes no difference—I enjoy engaging with people who are willing to engage with me.

A blitz is an intense concentration of activity. The Two Weeks to a Breakthrough program includes three blitzes: a share blitz, an action blitz, and a request blitz. Today, the focus is on sharing. Some of you might be thinking, "Share? I have been sharing for three days; I don't know who else to share with!" Trust me, you have just scratched the surface of sharing. Go to the next deeper level of individuals and groups around you. Connect with at least five people today. Ten would be better. Schedule at least two follow-up conversations for another day. Contact at least one stranger (someone you have never met, perhaps a keeper of the knowledge, an author, teacher, or famous expert). Connect big today.

Don't eat lunch alone. Go out for a break after work with a pal. Invite someone for a latte and chat. Contact people you have met at association meetings. Look through the business cards you have collected and review your e-mail contacts list. Share what you are up to fully and openly and express sincere interest in their endeavors. Your singular focus today is to get the word out. Share, share, share.

Hesitant? What have you got to lose? What's the worst-case scenario? The worst thing that might happen (and it is not likely) is that the other person will show indifference to your goal or decline your request for the conversation. You can handle this. You are not dealing with the threat of a world war or the release of a pandemic virus. Breakthroughs will be faster and sweeter if you learn to accept apathy and rejection with energy and passion. Here's an example:

>   *Lisa:*   Mr. Black, I admire your work. My company is
>   going through a process using your system. I
>   know you are a very busy man, but I would love
>   fifteen minutes of your time to ask a couple of
>   questions about the process we are using. I would
>   be happy to call you on a day and at a time that
>   is convenient for you. If you prefer, you can call
>   me anytime at [number]. Is there a day and time
>   this month that might work for you?
>
>   *Mr. Black:*   I am sorry, I am much too busy. Good luck with
>   your process. Regards, Mr. Black
>
>   *Lisa:*   Mr. Black, I understand completely. Thank
>   you for your contribution to our field. We have
>   learned so much from your work! Warm
>   regards, Lisa

Sometimes, the Mr. Blacks of the world say no—but sometimes they say yes. It is wonderful when yes happens. If you share your goals broadly and attempt to engage many people in conversations, you will find people who can and will want to support your journey. Stephen Covey is famous for saying that in every communication exchange we have with someone, we have the opportunity to either add to or subtract from the relationship. Make sure that your communication, even with friends and family, adds to your relationships. Even when you are being turned down! Be a great listener and show a desire to be engaged.

What does it mean to share? Think back to when you were ten years old. Your mother told you to share your toys, candy, and maybe even your Kraft Mac n' Cheese. This usually meant ripping the candy bar in half or taking turns on the teeter-totter. The same goes with your process of sharing today. Sharing means that each party gets something. When you share what you are up to and ask people for their thoughts and ideas, you are giving them the opportunity to contribute to your success. People want to do this. It feels great. That said, make sure you are gracious and generous about offering your time back to them. I always conclude shares with an offer. For example:

- Hey, buddy, I owe you one. Please let me know anytime I can return the favor.
- Your input has been invaluable. I would be happy to reciprocate anytime.
- What can I do for you?
- You mentioned that you were up to your eyeballs in alligators—can I help you with anything?
- You have been a great sounding board for me. Let me know if there is anything that you would like to bounce off me before going live; I would be happy to help.

And always end with sincere thanks.

- You've made a big difference, thanks so much.
- I love your idea, thanks a million.
- It means a lot to get your thoughts on this.
- I know you are super busy, so thanks for taking the time!

When people feel that you are grateful and that they made a difference for you, they feel great. That's sharing.

It is important that you listen when you share. This sounds counterintuitive, but the magic of sharing is in hearing and seeing how people react to your goal. To make big things happen, listen well. The catalysts for most breakthroughs come from other people out there, so it's dangerous to miss a thing! Active listening is a way of listening and responding that improves mutual understanding.

Many people are poor listeners. They get distracted, talk too much, and think about what they are going to say next when they should be listening. They assume that they know what the other person is going to say and tune them out. It can be difficult to take the time and energy to listen actively, but the rewards are worth the effort. You are listening actively when you

- Have a sincere interest in the other person and pay attention. Lean in during the conversation and treat everyone as if they were among the thinkers you admire most.
- Are open to diverse points of view and coachable (which means you can be influenced).
- Demonstrate that you are interested in hearing the other person's point of view.
- Are nonjudgmental and seek to understand diverse points of view without being critical.
- Focus on the conversation and resist distractions in the environment.
- Are able to confirm what you've heard.
- Reflect on the ideas, suggestions, and concerns that others offer.
- Ask substantive provocative and evocative questions to gain deeper layers of understanding.
- Allow others to do the talking and refrain from jumping into the conversation too quickly.

How does this apply to e-mail? It's easy to get distracted when reading e-mail, just like when someone else is talking (looking around, thinking about what you need to get done, singing along with the radio, and so on). When we don't pay attention to what people are communicating, we are not sharing well. The feedback we need to make a breakthrough is out there. Will we hear it? I am challenged with this all the time and have to remind myself to reflect on and consider the gifts people are offering me in the form of feedback, coaching, and input.

Your three daily challenges:

- Where am I lacking follow-up? Follow up today!
- Am I listening? Ask this several times today.
- With whom should I connect? Connect today.

Flap, flap, flap.
From past program participants . . .

I am sorry I have been so quiet the last few days, but my excuse is valid. I have been inundated with excitement, replies and booked appointments from my three public talks. Since last Friday evening, I have been averaging around four hours sleep a night. Not in my wildest dreams did I expect a response like this. I have created a problem for myself in that I cannot serve all the clients that need my services. I switched my requests to medical and other related professionals for assistance in their fields. Those that have replied said that they had been contacted by people who had attended my talks and were keen to partner with me.

The opportunities this provides me with are staggering. I can now visibly position myself as one of the top experts in the field. I introduce and appear alongside the top medical and alternative-medicine minds available, I get immediate exposure to at least a third of the doctors and specialists in Southern Africa—which is my referral base—as well as potential sponsors. I also want to be able to promote my book at the same time.

The daily action is so important. I hadn't even realized what enormous amounts of progress could be made by just putting my thoughts out to the universe instead of walking around with them thinking—"Mr. XYZ must have had the right contacts to pull off what he did."

There are many other benefits that I have received from the program, not the least of which is sharing my goals. The responses and the reactions are good, but the act and process of sharing the goal and experiences are really good.

## Thursday, Day Five: Fresh Eyes

Today's daily practice is one share, two requests, and three actions. Are you still doing your daily practice? If you are drawing a blank on what to do, return to your Priming the Pump worksheet. The exercise for today is to look at your project or goal from a variety of perspectives and filters. How would the following people view your goal, progress, and barriers?

- Friends
- Peers
- Managers
- Customers
- Competitors
- Vendors
- Partners
- Industry experts
- Coaches and counselors

Can you see these other perspectives? How might others assess and address the barriers that are getting in the way, or may be doing so? What ideas might they think of that you have not? If you are producing written materials, do your words capture the needs, interests, and ideas of these various readers? Have you answered the questions that they are likely to ask? Are you appealing to readers based on their preferences, styles, and voice—or yours? If you are a leader, are you seeing the goal as your peers, employees, and managers would? If you are not sure, ask.

Think of contextual changes that might help expand your thinking. Try a change of place, setting, schedule, habit, or network. The winds of the world will carry you to success if you flap your butterfly wings enough and with focus and passion. Use your daily practice to see your goal with a fresh set of eyes. Have a spectacular day!

Your three daily challenges:

- Which perspective is most foreign to me and how can I understand it?
- Who is the biggest naysayer and what can I learn from that point of view?
- What setting or context change might help me see things with new eyes?

Flap, flap, flap.

From past program participants . . .

I did make a very large request on Thursday—I asked for a job and a generous compensation package. Then I bit my nails for 36 hours. Then, I got it! The coolest thing about this opportunity is that it lines up with my goals in terms of what I have flushed out in this process so far. Lisa's questions about what full engagement has looked like in the past, what it means to be contributing, and the other questions that forced me to think about why I want to move in the direction I want to move were helpful. My doubting mind wanted to take over and focus on fear, unknown, potential failure, etc. But doing this work pointed me back to the bigger picture of what I want—beyond any job or any compensation. To be surrounded by people that share my values and that take actions in alignment with those values—that's what I want. And I want it to be present in all areas of my life, not just personal friendships or spiritual circles. That is a HUGE ah-ha for me.

Today, I am enjoying this perspectives part of the game. I have talked with more than three people today and the biggest perspective that I am being reminded of so far is gratitude. Gratitude for what has been, what is and what is to come. It is amazing how different I feel—how much more positive and light—when I am focused on gratitude rather than resentment or faults in others. I'll continue to shift perspectives through the day!

## Friday, Day Six: What If?

Today's daily practice is one share, two requests, and three actions. You should start seeing a natural shift from sharing to requests. Although sharing is never over, you will have more substantive requests to make after you have explored your goal and received feedback and ideas from others. When you share your goal, you should be asking people to recommend others you ought to know. Follow up and request fifteen-minute meet-and-greet conversations with these people.

The theme for today is fun and challenging. To create more ideas, angles, ways, perspectives, possibilities, and approaches relative to your goal, ask at least a dozen what-if questions like these:

- What if time were not an issue?
- What if I knew _____?
- What if I cleared my calendar today?
- What if I am talking to the wrong people?
- What if I viewed this from the customer's perspective?
- What if I partnered with someone? Who would that be? What would I say? What would it mean?
- What if I need to create a support structure, how might I do this?
- What if today were two years from now? How have things changed?
- What if technology X takes off?
- What if I asked for exactly what I want?
- What if I am barking up the wrong tree?
- What if my goal were achieved, how would I feel? What would things look like?
- What if the answer is right in front of me?

Ask two friends to help you brainstorm what-if questions and the answers. Be in the land of what-if today. Make one or two of these what-ifs a reality. Clear your calendar, ask for what you want, bark up the right tree.

Your three daily challenges:

- How might I generate an invigorating and challenging list of what-if questions?
- What can I do to expand my thinking?
- Which one what-if scenario would make the greatest difference today?

Flap, flap, flap.
From past program participants . . .

In the past couple of days, I have shared my goal with around 20 people, two of which could be influential down the road. In addition, I have gotten agreement from one of them to take my cause to a key industry-influencing group that he's part of. Sometimes the two shares a day approach seems mechanical, but when I look back on the week, I got more done than I expected. Nice when that happens.

I must admit I was a little reluctant to go through all the questions at first. It seemed like I already had a great bunch of ideas and lots of people to talk to. But actually, the questions helped shape some of my ideas, and encouraged me to think even bigger. Coming out of my answers, I can see two actions, five requests and five enhancements/refinements to the scope, as well as getting a vision for where this could go if it was wildly successful. And it has deepened my understanding of the idea, the benefits and the kind of information I need to know/asking when talking with all those people I made a request of!

Earlier this evening I was invited to hijack (sounds silly but it is true) a talk on ADD to some forty people. I grabbed the opportunity with everything I could. I had taken around thirty business cards—I didn't have enough. There is a good lesson to be learned from this. I nearly didn't go—I had to travel a considerable distance in stormy weather and I set out late. But I realized that even if I only managed to sign up one person, that is one less person I have to reach, but more importantly, I needed to convince that person to become a salesperson for me. My investment in being disciplined has already paid for itself. My first goal is to have a small group up and running within the two weeks. After tonight's event, I have the core of the group, now I have to create and deliver the content for them to use in the group over the next few weeks.

## Saturday, Day Seven: Analysis

> The unexamined life is not worth living.
>
> —*Socrates*

For your daily practice, do one quick action, one reflection, and one mind exercise. If you have been doing your daily practice and exploring daily themes, you have been uncovering new rocks and generating lots of data and ideas related to your goal. Take some time today to see what you have learned so far. Evaluate where you should take your actions, shares, and requests during the second week of the program. What do you still want to learn? What is your data telling you? Where is it leading you? Is it a direction you want to explore? Try generating burning questions—the ones that start with, "I really wish I knew" or "If only I could find out." Determine who might be able to answer these questions and plan to ask them in the next couple days. Record your assumptions, conclusions, and questions, and record these in the Priming the Pump worksheet for use next week.

Think about the last six days. What barriers keep popping up again and again? Are these barriers that have plagued you for years? Another kind of analysis for today is to think about what you have learned about your style and automatic habits and how these either help or get in the way of achieving your goals. Take a look at the belief/action cycle, shown in Figure 4.

*Beliefs-actions-results*. Your beliefs determine your actions, which determine your results. When you want to create a breakthrough, you use the model in reverse, asking yourself first, What results do you seek? Then, based on your desired results, What actions will best support achieving your goal? Finally, based on the actions that support the goal, Which beliefs should you adopt? What would be most helpful? To change your results, you might need to adopt some new beliefs and let go of some old ones. When I work with coaching clients, it is common that what's holding them back is their beliefs. When they align their beliefs to support their goals, whammo, they zoom forward.

Today is also the day to begin blowing the lid off your results by spending time connecting in a new way. Put your head in a different space. Be positive, caring, giving, and resolute about your goal. Talk about it in "this shall be" terms. Plan the big plays.

If you have a habit that gets in the way (procrastination, getting stalled by overwhelm, resistance to involving others, or anything else) it's likely you have beliefs that trigger these responses. I do not know what your beliefs are, but here are a few common examples:

*Beliefs that lead to procrastination:* I can perform well enough leaving things to the last minute. I need to think about this more.

## Figure 4.  The Belief/Action Cycle.

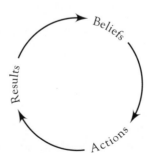

This is not important. I am afraid of not getting this right. If I am smart enough, I can do this with little prep or planning. I don't want to be responsible or mature. As long as I have not given it my full attention, I am protected from feelings of failure.

*Beliefs that lead to becoming stalled by overwhelm:* If I think about it for a while, things will sort themselves out. If I play the victim, I don't have to face responsibility. Nobody should have to deal with this much stuff! It is better to fail by not finishing than to pour my heart and mind into this and fail.

*Beliefs that lead to resistance to involving others:* If I do not engage others, I cannot be rejected. I need to be right; I need to be in charge. People are not interested in what I am doing. I want to do this on my own.

These are just examples—I'm not suggesting that any of these beliefs must apply to you. Once you have explored the beliefs underlying your sources of resistance, think about and adopt alternative beliefs that would better serve your goal. Try acting as though you have that belief for the next week and see what happens. For example, here are some alternative beliefs for the obstructive ones:

- If I want to achieve this goal, I need to be willing to step outside my comfort zone and stay in focused action.
- The greatest failure is giving up on what I am passionate about—not trying—not giving it my best shot.
- Success is living full out and engaging people in my goals. The best results will come when I enroll others.
- While there's a lot going on, I can tame this beast and focus on what's most important. I will not let the details and to-do lists suck me under!

You get the idea. You need to create the beliefs that work for you and then identify actions you can begin to take today that are consistent with this belief. Record these new actions on your list for next week.

Analysis of stuff.
Analysis within.
Enjoy this reflection.
Your three daily challenges:

- What are my burning questions?
- What beliefs are not serving my goals? If you are not zooming along, then you have beliefs that are not serving you well.
- What small action might make a big difference?

Flap, flap, flap.
From past program participants . . .

Acknowledging barriers helped me to increase my focus. I have a tendency to be a stargazer before I start something. Once I start moving, though, I tend to lose myself in the details and become a victim (many actions, but no focus). By acknowledging and listing the barriers, I could increase my focus and at the same time maintain the correct actions.

The Belief/Action cycle is so important. I didn't believe (pun not intended) till I saw the simplicity in the diagrams. Every day I had a few hundred thousand excuses on why I wasn't getting out and doing what I always thought I was supposed to be doing—generating revenue to my fullest potential—back then they seemed like genuine obstacles or things that needed to be handled first. Now they seem like excuses, reasons for me to stay in the safe zone, in the security and warmth that I was afraid to leave. Strange how a simple change in ideas can drastically change the actions that we perform.

Looking at today's e-mail what stood out for me was that I have a nasty cocktail of some of each of the types of beliefs going on with several of my projects that feed into this goal—I'm not trying to fit myself into the potential examples for the sake of it—I looked at them and they glared out at me from the page: it varies of course, but my usual tipple seems to be a combination of "As long as I have not given it my full attention, I am protected from feelings of failure" + "it is better to fail by not finishing than to pour my heart and mind into this and fail" + "people are not interested in what I am doing." So what would the alternative beliefs be that would serve my goal better? 1) I can trust myself not to fail—my ideas about this area are well informed and I've thought them through more than anyone else tackling this area in the organization so why not? (A belief that my boss is very keen that I take on but that I have been resisting). 2) My colleagues have recently expressed concerns at their abilities to get everything they need to get done and they are working to challenging deadlines—they would appreciate a helping hand (without the need to take classes!) and that is what I have on offer—they'd be mad not to be interested! I think those two beliefs come from the heart and that I have a fighting chance at sticking to them for the next week. I've had various moments when I've been asked to/given an opportunity to examine unhelpful beliefs and I've always shied away from it and/or drawn a blank. Somehow today it flowed naturally and what I have come up with feels real rather than the product of a contrived exercise. I reckon I do already believe the new beliefs.

## Sunday, Day Eight: Wild Ideas

You have arrived at Day Eight, wow. Today's daily practice is thinking of wild ideas! Happy Sunday. Sunday is a great day to relax and reflect. Today you will prepare your body and mind for the coming week. For now, take stock of your riches and let your mind dream. This is going to be fun!

Wild idea: Something beyond the normal, reasonable, and average. Today, I'd like you to identify and place a $2 bet on a few long shots (like the one that won the Kentucky Derby in 2005, Giacomo, a 50-1 long shot, where a $2 bet earned $102). Think about your project and all the ideas you have come up with over the last seven days. Did you think of and dismiss any wild ideas? Here are a few prompts to help you think of wild ideas:

- List a partnership that would be just too good to be true.
- List a sponsor that you think would be a long shot.
- Who, in your wildest dreams, would you like to hear pitching or telling others about you and your work?
- If you could have any job, contract, or project, what would it be?
- If you were feeling really brave and confident, what requests would you make? Make them on Monday!
- List one dream appointment. Request it on Monday.

Wild ideas are a numbers game, so try more than one next week. If you give ten wild ideas a try, I bet you will have a major, Alaska-sized breakthrough. Share your wild ideas with a friend and ask them to contribute five more wild ideas. Go wild!

As well as thinking wild, make sure that you have a list of requests you can make on Monday during the requests blitz (yes, this is advance warning). Oh, what fun it will be! (It can be a lot of fun.)

Your three daily challenges:

- Which wild idea makes me tingle all over? (Do that one tomorrow—or today.)
- Am I thinking wild enough? What can I do to generate wild ideas?
- Which wild idea would my hero jump on?

Flap, flap, flap.
From past program participants . . .

I have mine, and am planning on how to do it for Monday. Not so much a wild idea, but a go big or stay home request I've been putting off for a while. I will make the call on Monday, and I have the script for the pitch. I'm going for it.

My wild idea is that I can write a proposal that will win a multimillion-Euro consulting contract and deliver that proposal by telephone tomorrow night to an audience in Moscow who will be evaluating my proposal through an interpreter. At the same time, I will find a chunk of time to take all the feedback I received from my group of advisors to rewrite the e-mail broadcast to 20,000 prospects on Tuesday. I will also find another chunk of time to implement Joshua's suggestion to organize an urgent order fire drill for my staff on Monday.

## Monday, Day Nine: Requests Blitz

Today's daily practice is requests. I love doing requests blitzes—I still do them once a month or so and almost always make great things happen. Really! Monday is a great day of the week to make requests because people have enough time to respond before the week ends. Play big today. If you have not been rockin' and rollin' with requests, today is the day to make things happen. Remember, requests can cover a broad variety of topics and needs. Here are a couple of inspiring blog posts about requests.

### Ask for What You Want

*By Dick Richards, Come Gather Round Blog, May 21, 2005*

A weekend leadership seminar in Northern Ireland. The dozen or so participants are owners of small to medium sized companies, senior managers from a major corporation, and assorted others including a Catholic nun. The seminar is part of a business school's Master of Science in Leadership program. The man who directs the program noticed that his students often failed to ask directly for what they want—not good if you desire to lead. He asked me (I am leading the seminar) to address the issue.

We sit in a circle and discuss the difficulty of asking for what you want, the whys and hows of doing so, and then I suggest that we practice. The first few people to speak ask for what you would expect. "I want new accounts for the business." "I want more energy from my people." It is the nun's turn. She says, "I want someone to give me a house." The group is stunned by the direct, specific request. It seems improbable: who gives houses away? It also seems audacious and absurd!

The man sitting next to her asks why she wants a house. She explains that she wants to set up a shelter for mothers and children who need a temporary place to live. He tells her, "I have several houses that I need to get rid of. You can have one; two if you want them." His company purchased a property on which he intends to build a plant. There was a row of abandoned houses along the edge of the property. He is renovating and selling them. He is offering to give her one or two newly renovated houses.

For the second time in just a few minutes, the group is stunned. The exchange between the man and the nun is a dramatic demonstration of what we talked about during our discussion: that you have a much better chance of getting what you want if you ask for it, and if you ask in a direct and specific way. Also that doing so is an indicator of strength rather than weakness: the others recognize her request as an act of courage.

So let's practice. I'll go first. I want at least a million people, including you, to read my next book within the first year of publication. (The book—Is Your Genius At Work?—will be released this coming November). Your turn. Use the comment link below, and remember: direct and specific. P.S. I don't have any houses to give away.

Great story, right? Imagine the feeling the nun had. And what about the man who donated the houses? He was probably feeling great as well. Requests that come from the heart and seek to improve lives are a win-win. Here is another inspiring and entertaining blog post about the power of requests:

## For My Next Trick

*By Fred Gratzon, The Lazy Way to Success, May 13, 2005*

Inspired and stunned by the weekend's sports news that golf pro Sergio Garcia incomprehensibly blew a 6-stroke lead going into the final round of the Wachovia Classic Championship, I thought I'd write another book. I bounced the idea off a friend. The premise is that the mind can, on one hand, be an enormous asset in an athletic performance and, on the other, interfere with a performance and screw things up no matter how hard you practiced. I told my friend that I wanted to interview top athletes to find out the ways they get their minds right.

If you have been a regular reader, you know that back in February I wrote about athletic performance and the Zone. (Check out February's archives for the 14th, 15th, 17th and 28th.)

My friend loved the idea but said the problem was getting access to the athletes. I had to agree and felt deflated. However, that evening (the night before the Day of Lasting Achievements) I made a list of all the things I wanted to pursue on May 10 in order to take maximum advantage of that auspicious day. During that list-making exercise, I happened to think of three or four of my friends that had some connection with professional athletes.

When Akshaya Tritiya (The Day of Lasting Achievements) dawned I called some and emailed the others. Miraculously, a book customer called (out of the blue) to order a bunch of my books to give out as gifts. It turned out he was the son of a majorly famous (and now quite old) tennis pro. He loved the idea and said he'd open some doors for me. The few friends I contacted sprang into action too. Now I have some phone numbers (even cell numbers) for a couple of very cool superstars. Hopefully one thing will lead to another.

I'm stoked to the gills. We'll see how it unfolds. I'll keep you all up to date if anything worth reporting takes place. Right now, even at age 59, I'm feeling like a little kid again. I'm going to ask some questions that I always wanted to know from these hugely accomplished athletes and I can't wait.

P.S. Of course, if any of you could introduce me to a great athlete (or if you are a great athlete), please get in touch with me.

Oh, the power of requests backed up by passion and drive! Today is your day to focus on harnessing the potential of requests. Requests can cover a lot of territory but should focus on moving your goal forward. Consider making requests that pertain to:

- Creating more time for yourself, your schedule, or your project.
- Asking people to meet with you and let you pick their brains.
- Asking people to participate in your project.
- Asking for financial support, like sponsorship, advertising, or a sale of a product or service.
- Improving your skills or effectiveness.
- Asking people to barter with you.
- Asking people to make an introduction on your behalf.
- Asking a group of people to help you brainstorm, think through, or plan your project.
- Asking people to review and critique your plan.
- Asking people to be your evangelists (like asking them to blog about you and your project, or to send an announcement to their e-mail network).
- Asking local, regional, or national press for coverage—a mention or an article.
- Asking for help on other projects so you can concentrate on this one.
- Asking for a job interview or informal meeting.
- Asking for a brief meeting to share how you think you can help company X meet or beat its goals.
- Improving your finances (lower credit card rates, renegotiate bills, sell excess items, get business loans).

List and make ten requests today. Making requests in person is best because doing so puts your goal more powerfully in the world and the person is more likely to grant the request or offer some assistance. Requesting by phone is second best and e-mail or mail is a third option. Use all three methods for delivering requests. If you need help formulating requests, review Chapter Four again.

A reminder: I have found it helpful to let people know up front that they should feel no pressure to say yes, that you will still be their biggest fan and friend no matter what they say, that they should not feel uncomfortable if the answer is no, and that you would be thrilled if they said yes. Always thank people for their consideration. This is important for maintaining the long-term relationship. You should build your skill and comfort for responding to no. Get even better at accepting a yes!

The requests blitz can be the most transforming day of the program. If you are having a hard time coming up with a robust and inspiring list, ask a friend to help and review the themes for the last few days (they were designed to generate ideas for requests). If just one of your ten requests is granted, things will be different and great. Breakthroughs will follow!

Your three daily challenges:

- Which requests are most important to the success of my goal?
- How can I make requests a win-win situation?
- How can I make sure that I respond to both yeses and nos in ways that will make people feel good?

Flap, flap, flap.
From past program participants . . .

And Lisa, thanks for the program, and especially the bit in today's goal where you said in person is best. Just being able to go up to someone and ask like I did today is something I've NEVER been able to do before, but every time I felt like putting it off, those words kept coming back to haunt me!

I finally got to 10 requests. Whew! I didn't want to give myself credit for puny little requests, so it's been a challenge getting to 10 that qualify. I found a bit of fear of success clouding my judgment—how bizarre! This is going to be interesting, no matter which way the requests go.

I made eight requests in the last two days. It feels good. Also, I just got back from a fantastic road trip with a friend so had time to share what I'm working on toward my breakthrough with her as well. I'm feeling extreme productivity!

## Tuesday, Day Ten: Playing and Planning

Today's daily practice is one share, one request, and four actions. I would like you to reconnect with your goal. Say it to yourself. Is it compelling? Does it still excite you and make the hair on the back of your neck stand up? Notice how you have reshaped your thinking over the last week. Play around with expressing your goal a few different ways until you have two or three crisp one-line explanations of your goal. This exercise gives you more ammunition for sharing with others and may help you further refine your goal. Challenge yourself—is this the goal worthy of your time and passion? Make sure you are focused on the goal and not on one action within the goal. For example, one program participant had a goal of starting a coaching business. Throughout the program, she remained focused on one project that supported that goal, getting a Web site up and running. While this task needed to be done, she struggled with a bit of tunnel vision and lost a few opportunities to make the Web site sing and express her larger goal of having an amazing coaching practice that facilitated other people's breakthroughs. She was defining her success in terms of numbers of Web pages written instead of content that expressed her passion and unique products and services.

Let's play a little basketball. (You remember basketball, right?) To play, we need to get on the court. You have five days left in the program. Your opponent is tough, has been practicing for years, and has been well fed. (Your opponent is your habits, beliefs, fears, resistance.) I don't know what your score is right now, as it will be different for each program participant. And here's the thing—it does not matter. You can still win, even if you have been asleep on the bench (or in the stands).

If you have made it this far, you have probably been playing on the court at least some of the time. What's your game plan? What plays and maneuvers will ensure that you win over your opponent? You can score only if you remember to dribble, focus, shoot, and follow through. Take some time today to redeclare your goals and to plan your plays. Have fun with it. Make sure your thoughts and ideas are on the court. Conditioning and skill are important, but the difference between winning and losing is often a head game. This applies to sports, business, family life, and hobbies.

Tomorrow is the action blitz—so plan now. Write down ten small actions, or three large ones, that you can, should, and will make on Day Eleven. Go ahead and do at least one of those today, to get a head start. Add one more to the list. Trust me, this works. If you can't think of at least twenty-five potential actions, you are being too narrow or conservative. The more the merrier and the bigger the better!

Your three daily challenges:

- Who's winning the game—my opponent or me? Why?
- Which four small actions will best prepare me for a great action blitz tomorrow?
- Can I capture the essence of my goal in one or two lines that anyone would understand?

Flap, flap, flap.
From past program participants . . .

I have learned so much in the past two weeks. Part of what I learned is that I have a tendency to say yes to more than is reasonable or realistic. To be totally honest, I have not been diligent about this process.

I have still experienced breakthroughs in my thinking and in my actions. I have saved everything from each of the days so I can try again on my own. I don't feel that I worked the program to the degree necessary to experience the true breakthrough results that are possible.

"Drowning in resistance?" Heh. My opponent is indeed tough. But the action of taking action, even if indirectly related, is helping make it easier to keep taking action. It's hard for me to get to all actions, shares, and requests every day but every action adds up and makes it easier.

I liked the playing with my goal today. It gave me some additional options when it comes to sharing, which is something I'm still finding a bit challenging.

## Wednesday, Day Eleven: Action Blitz

Today's daily practice: *ten actions* in support of your goal! You read that right—ten. Before you get worried, consider this. You have many little things to follow up on:

- Thoughts from the weekend
- People to get back to
- Flyers to drop off
- Content to proof
- E-mail to send
- Internet research to complete
- Requests to deliver
- Meetings to call
- Offices to organize
- Brainstorming sessions to conduct
- Applications to complete
- Ideas to explore
- Successes to celebrate
- Plans to create
- Benchmarking to do and competition to check out

You get the idea. Make today a day for being unstoppable. Little actions. Quick actions. Big actions. Do you have five minutes between meetings? Get two small actions done in that time. Do you have just a minute until you need to leave? Get one thing done. Make big things happen in small pockets of time.

Focused actions create pace and energy. An extraordinarily productive day will infuse your goal with fire and light. You can get caught up and more today if you play full out. Ready, set, *go-go-go*.

Your three daily challenges:

- How can I arrange my day so I can be unstoppable?
- Which actions will make the greatest difference?
  Do these first.
- How can I use tiny pockets of time to improve my pace and results?

Flap, flap, flap.
From a past program participant . . .

The day got off to a less than perfect start as I traveled to work on a packed train which pulled out of the station with the doors still open (that shouldn't be physically possible) and someone nearly fell out, but I pulled the emergency stop cord and was a hero for a few brief seconds. Once I caught up from the ensuing delays everything has been going swimmingly. My 1-to-1 meeting went fine and I felt that I was much more able to express my enthusiasm about my projects and felt much more on my boss's wavelength than I have been for a while. Actions:

1. Met with Nick.
2. Talked through and got agreement on my innovation program proposal.
3. Sent follow-up e-mail to Nick with the good news.
4. Looked for venue options.
5. Followed up with thank yous for the replies I got from my requests for book reviews (and I got some more yeses!).

6. Asked my boss if she would consider me working a two-day week starting later in the year if I put together a business case and she said that she'd consider it (no promises, but I wouldn't expect that anyway).

7. Shared more about my goal with my boss—she's very interested and keen to hear about how the two weeks pan out.

8. Mentioned my goal to a new manager who I was briefing about my role today—she is all for it and has pledged her support.

9. Read a review of a software tool that could be a good add-on tool for my innovation team and put a reminder to download the trial version on PC at home.

10. Read e-mail which arrived from one of the keepers of the current wisdom with a summary of research on training effectiveness which was quite sobering and encouraging at the same time.

I had more planned but was pulled in to do a last-minute presentation at our end of year celebration (we beat our fundraising budget this year and have growth ahead of the average in the sector—hooray! Now let's see what they can do this year with all the extra informal learning I'm going to encourage). I didn't let the bad journey in stop me and managed to fit in an awful lot of actions to an already packed day—I think it qualified as an unstoppable day. (Apart from the train—that really needed to stop). The major breakthrough was getting to the point where I can go full on with my innovation program and I no longer feel scared of it—my belief in trusting myself is really working, mainly by preventing procrastination born of fear of failure. I'm really finding this immensely valuable.

## Thursday, Day Twelve: Giving Back

Today's daily practice is one share, one request, and two actions. One way to experience a breakthrough is by contributing to the success of others. And I don't mean helping others so you can gain. When we sincerely offer our time, minds, and hearts, we gain and grow. Think of a few ways in which you can give back today. How could you make a difference for others? What could you offer that would mean a lot to someone else? How might you volunteer? What could you do that would be a welcomed surprise? How might you help someone else produce a breakthrough today?

Compose two or three e-mails or make phone calls offering to contribute to others (or better yet, offer in person). It will be most meaningful if you offer to assist business acquaintances or non-profit organizations. You can help out your friends, too, but this is something you probably already do. It's even better to contribute in new ways.

This is a great exercise because it illustrates the power of contribution. It feels great to help others. Keep this in mind when making requests. If you are sharing of yourself and talking about your goal in open and compelling terms, people will want to contribute to your success. It will feel great for them, just like giving back feels great to you. The second reason I like this exercise is that it allows you to experience another context and perspective. Your requests and actions today can relate to your goal or to your contribution to others in general.

Your three daily challenges:

- Is there a small thing I could do right now that would make a big difference to someone else?
- If I could help anyone or any cause, what would I do? Do it.
- How can I learn from helping others?

Flap, flap, flap.
From past program participants . . .

This is really hard to think about right now. So much is going on, I get a little overwhelmed just thinking of volunteering to help someone else. Maybe I'll offer to help, but find out what I can do toward the end of July or something. [Posted the next morning . . . ] I did something after all. I offered to (and did) rewrite a marketing letter for a nonprofit org I am working with (which actually relates to my goal, oddly enough). Look—the stars—they are aligning!

I have a result regarding the giving back theme last week. I e-mailed friends and family about joining a fundraising campaign and not only has my sister-in-law signed up, but she told her internal colleagues about it. They are putting it on their intranet and in various in-house newsletters. It could be seen by thousands of people as her employer is the biggest in their area! From small seeds . . .

## Friday, Day Thirteen: Being It Today

> Be the change you wish to see in the world.
>
> —*Gandhi*

Today's daily practice is one share, one request, and two actions. Wow, we are almost to the end of the program (it's only beginning in some respects). Let's make these last two days the best yet! Are you still doing your daily practice? If you are drawing a blank on what to do, revisit your Priming the Pump worksheet. This is one of my favorite days of the program (the request blitz is my top favorite). You have had some time to explore and play around with your goal, but are you being it? If your goal is to build a successful business, are you thinking and acting like a successful business-person? If your goal is to finish a book, are you thinking and acting like a successful author? If your goal is to get a great new job or contract, are you thinking and acting like the successful people who have held this role in the past?

Create and take on the persona that will serve your goals! Think about the beliefs, habits, associations, and style that will be most helpful to you. This is something you can have fun with. Begin by recognizing yourself in association with your goal. I'm a break-through catalyst, business writer, and management and leadership consultant. That's me. Do I have a Ph.D. in this? No. Are there other worthy experts and people with interesting ideas and perspectives? Absolutely. Does this mean I am not a worthy professional?

No! How about you? Practice describing yourself consistent with your goal.

- I am an entrepreneur in the area of online business development.
- I am a professional leader.
- I am bilingual in English and French.
- I am a master problem solver.
- I am a professional musician.
- I am a Web site developer.
- I am a chef.
- I am a world explorer.

How does it sound? How does it feel? Send a note to your team saying who you are being. Approach today with your head held high and ready to conquer the world!

Your three daily challenges:

- Am I being the change I seek in my world?
- Who can I be that would best serve my goals?
- How might my biggest fan describe me?

Flap, flap, flap.

From past program participants . . .

I've already put today's suggestion into action—I introduce myself to potential clients as a Web design and usability consultant. It seems initially strange, but it's a genuine description of what I already do. Look at a bus driver. What they do is written right there in their job title. There's nothing strange and unquantifiable about that, and it's just the same for my title: I'm consulted on Web design and usability. I don't want or need to embellish it!

What fun, Lisa! I'm having a blast being a published author today.

### Saturday, Day Fourteen: Thanks and Reflection

Today's daily practice is one share, one request, and two actions. It is Day Fourteen—can you believe it? I want to thank you for participating in this program. Each time someone makes it to the end of the two-week program, I feel like my butterfly wings have flapped one more time, and it is gratifying. Some readers will be more active than others, but that's fine and normal. My goal is for each one to experience excellent progress and several breakthroughs.

The theme for Day Fourteen is thanks and reflection. If you're like most participants, your work on your goals will continue. Even so, it's a good time to

- Reflect on the two-week process. Think about your progress and where you came from. Acknowledge what you have learned about your goal and yourself.

- Thank those who have contributed to your exploration and assisted you during the process.

- Acknowledge your breakthroughs and celebrate your successes. Remember, breakthroughs are anything that helps you skip forward. Did you experience any ah-has or have lightbulb moments?

## What's Next?

You want to keep your momentum going strong. You can do it! Here are a few ideas for what's next. Keep on doing the program! Apply the techniques that worked well for you and act like the program is starting again. In April 2006 I had a group go through the program and three of the participants decided to start over immediately and keep updating each other using a Google e-mail group. Chapter Six offers several ways you can customize the program to fit your goal, situation, and preferred work style. Take a break for a couple of days, then readopt the daily practice to maintain your focus and action. Create your own daily practice.

Your three daily challenges:

- How can I keep my momentum going without burning out or getting bored?
- If I created my own daily practice, what would it look like?
- How can I best show appreciation to those who have helped me get his far?

Flap, flap, flap.
From past program participants . . .

I never expected to get as much out of this program as I did, and I'm very glad I got the chance to take part. I experienced lots of breakthroughs in various areas, and I'm definitely coming out of it more aware of how to make my goal happen. My favorite part of the program was when I finally started getting results! The hardest part was pushing myself to make the efforts that led to the results.

### My main take-aways from this process:

I reaffirmed the importance of specific, written goals.

I realized the power of small, persistent actions toward a goal.

I discovered the effectiveness of asking/allowing someone else to poke me daily to keep me focused on my goal.

I found I could make far more progress in two weeks than I'd ever have thought possible.

I confirmed that discipline is not just a choice—it's a bunch of choices and opportunities—if you missed one opportunity, get right back on track by seizing the next.

This process reminded me of something a friend of mine once told me: "If you figure out what you really want, and ask for it, you just might get it." The breakthroughs are ours for the taking.

I have just posted an e-mail about how well the daily practice and connecting with other people in my network has gone. A phone call to a former client following a vicious jab of conscience resulted in me being asked to arrange a two-hour closed Cable TV broadcast to 3,600 doctors and specialists on my topic on any Tuesday in July. I get to choose the panel participants, and have final say on the agenda. I am able to position myself alongside the best minds in the country, and in one fell swoop, I get exposure to 3,600 eager medical eyeballs of my source of referrals. I am a part owner of the content, so we will be creating DVD productions aimed at different market segments from the original broadcast footage, to sell into the professional, train-the-trainer market, and of course into the consumer market. As the professional market covers the bottom half of Africa, we can utilize the capability of DVD and do the productions in eight different languages. This Two Weeks to a Breakthrough program really rocks—the value of daily practice implemented passionately is proving to be a wonderful investment.

Did you make it through the program? Hip hip hooray if you did. It takes drive, resolve, and passion to make big things happen. In the next chapter, I share ideas for how to customize the program. I recommend doing the two-week program once as defined here before you tackle redesigning the program. The two-week format has something special and magical. It's long enough for big things to happen and short enough that most people can commit to it fully.

Now luxuriate in your victory. Smile.

Flap, flap, flap.

# 6

# CONCLUSION

You are amazing. I know this! If you and I were to settle down for a chat over foaming lattes, I am sure that your greatness would shine bright and I would find your hopes and dreams inspiring. Everyone I meet possesses clear and special talents. I love to discover the source of people's passions and am fascinated by our diverse natures.

Every night, we see people at their best—and more often their worst—on television news programs. If everyone is amazing, what's going on? I think that stress and the dizzying circumstances of our lives can push us off course. We know this is not how things ought to be. We know that we have something greater and more compelling to offer the world. Even so, we get farther off course with each mismatched turn. The butterfly effect goes negative with too many of these small steps off the path. They add up, add up, and soon we are miles away from where we intended.

You are amazing even if today you are off course. You have the potential to contribute to society and live a wonderful and fulfilling life. You can get back on track. I work with many people who choose to stop moving in the wrong direction and see a new set of possibilities. They flap their butterfly wings fast and furious, manifesting joy and wonder along the way. They ooze exuberance and become flexibly strong, like a tall Sequoia tree swaying in the wind. An awesome force of nature. What's your goal? Do you need an adjustment?

Dave from South Africa wanted to create a business that helps South Africans with adult ADD live better lives. He did that and more. Kathy wanted to manifest the job of her dreams. She asked for it and got it. Rob wanted to launch his own business creating

Web sites for small business owners. He's doing it. Donna wanted to create new possibilities for learning and development in the non-profit where she worked. She did. Dwayne wanted to expose a new set of potential customers to his firm's services. He's doing it. Scott wanted to help travel agents build their businesses through online communication and branding tools. The agents are signing up. Jackie wanted to create a plan that would help smart women get into and rise through the political process. She's doing it. Each person felt off course or stuck when they started the Two Weeks to a Breakthrough program but quickly began to move forward and in the right direction. Many small actions made a big difference and breakthroughs helped them to skip forward with velocity.

Pow. Zoom. Wowwee. Flap. You've read these words throughout this book. Am I just an excitable girl? No. This book and program are designed to help you create breakthrough results. Not good results and not great. Amazing! Results that deserve an exclamation point at the end. This simple stuff is powerful and magical. Magical because one day something new and wonderful appears. Seemingly out of nowhere, you manifest greatness. The suggestions in this book can be taken up by anyone. You can take them up, starting today. Take in the wonder of your world and get into focused action. Make your mark and let your passion and exuberance go wild. Break-throughs are waiting for you. It's your life to manifest.

Now that you have read about the program, I hope you give it a try. It works! Getting into focused action is what's most important, so feel free to adjust the program to fit your lifestyle. Here are a few ideas for ways you can customize the program.

- Try going through the program with a small group, even just one or two other people. Create an e-mail group and commit to reporting on your progress every day. Meet periodically to discuss your triumphs and areas of frustration or resistance. Hold one another accountable for completing the daily practice.

- This is a great program for intact work teams. Ask the training or OD department to facilitate morning huddles and create a communication and sharing forum.

- Some people want to take the weekends off. That's fine. Make it a fifteen-day program lasting three workweeks. Or take the second Friday off the program—anything goes!

- If you would like to be part of a group of people you don't know (there's safety in anonymity), I will have a place where people can connect on my Web site, www.lisahaneberg.com.

- If you want to try the program at a slower pace, you can try doing it every other day over four weeks. I recommend that you go for it and do the fourteen-day version, but doing it this way will work, too.

- Create your own daily practice. Start small with one share, one action, and one request. Add habits that will enable your success. Once you create your daily practice, block out time on your calendar every day.

This program is like a luscious ice-cream sundae. Combine the ingredients any way you like and it will still be delicious. Here are the ingredients:

- See, explore, and manifest new possibilities.
- Use breakthrough catalysts to make your journey easier.
- Create goals that stir your soul (nothing less).
- Harness the big power of small actions by doing your daily practice.
- Relish the journey and stay in focused action.

Flap, flap, flap.

# CASE STUDY

## Scott's Breakthrough Journal

Scott Ahlsmith is a travel business owner who joined the Two Weeks to a Breakthrough program to build customers and sales for a new service product called "You! the Brand." He went through an online version of the program that included daily e-mail from me with each day's theme and assignment (the same information you read in Chapter Five), an e-mail group that the participants could use to support one another, and three coaching conversations (at the beginning, middle, and end of the program).

Scott kept a journal of his experiences during the program. Here it is, in its entirety. I have crossed out names of people and companies to protect their privacy. When Scott uses the term *BKE*, he is referring to a breakthrough experience. At the end, I asked Scott to reflect on the experience. (That made him one of my "beloved guinea pigs"—people going through the program and keeping a more detailed journal on the process; when he uses *BGP*, that's what he means.)

Here is Scott's journal.

### Introduction

After a potpourri of undecided and undergraduate journalism, education, theater, and business courses, I settled into graduate school and got serious about computer science.

Well, not too serious. Before graduating, San Juan, PR [Puerto Rico] lured me to host a sales incentive trip for 80 Bissell Vacuum Cleaner representatives and their spouses. Seriously, you can't make-up stuff this good!

That was 35 years ago. Since then, I've enjoyed various travel industry gigs and have never felt like I "had to get up and go to work."

My goal: By December 31, 2006, I want more than 1,000 travel professionals paying an average of $35 a month for a new personal brand management service called, "YOU! the Brand."

The business opportunity for "YOU! the Brand." is valid because travelers want dependable, knowledgeable, and customized travel recommendations, yet most travel industry advertising promotes agencies, suppliers, products, and prices.

"YOU! the Brand." defines individual travel professionals, describes their expertise, and explains how this expertise enriches travelers' experiences while improving their bragging-rights when they return home.

I have a sleep-robbing passion for my goal because it clarifies the travel professional's emerging role and shows their evolution from commission-based agents-for-suppliers to consumer-focused advocates-for-travelers. After 35 years of travel industry experience, I have found something that I can "give back" to an industry that has given me so much.

My challenges:

Because "YOU! the Brand." is a new idea it has no basis for comparison. I feel scattered and frustrated. I have to explain the need for personal branding, teach the principles of branding, present the benefits of branding, explain the power of blogging and podcasting, and then overcome each prospect's "deer-in-headlights" silence or expression when my explanation misses the mark.

I feel a mile-wide and an inch-deep and believe 14-days of breakthrough coaching will help me gain clarity, purpose, and focus. At the same time, I believe many individuals with new business ideas will benefit from reading about my experiences and results.

My goal is important and interesting because:

My goal has universal appeal because it evolved from global events and technological innovations that have fundamentally changed nearly every business in today's economy. The changes that spawned my goal in tourism have similarly changed banking, manufacturing, insurance, investments, retail, and many others.

Fundamental change in a business creates chaos and chaos creates opportunities—especially for entrepreneurs. My goal takes advantage of chaotic business by applying blogging, podcasting and other viral marketing communication techniques with proven brand management strategies. The outcome restores personal business relationships (high touch) between buyers and sellers—tourists and travel professionals—and revitalizes productive marketplace conversations.

Achieving my goal and documenting the steps will provide a road map for others whose business goals are challenged by global events and technological innovations.

If only I could . . .

I don't know how to end a sentence that starts with those four words, because I know if I can picture the outcome, I can achieve it. I am so looking forward to sharing with and learning from each of you. Let's have some fun!

## Feedback Please

After my one-on-one teleconference with Lisa, we agreed to focus on resolving my main obstacle—crisply communicating what "YOU! the Brand." is and what it does for travel professionals. Below is the first e-promotion I broadcast to prospective customers a few weeks ago. It produced more questions than sales and unfortunately, relatively few questions!

*Would you please help me develop a more crisp and informative communication piece? What does this piece not tell you about "YOU! the Brand."? What questions does it raise? After seeing this promotional e-mail, what do you think "YOU! the Brand." does? How does it work? What else should I "fix"?*

*Thank you in advance for your frank and critical comments, Scott*

## Day 1—Sunday

How are you feeling today? Today is a travel day (Chicago to Ft Lauderdale) so I feel energetically focused. I need to make sure I have everything I need for the workshop (Fighting Discounting & Rebating) I'm presenting on Monday. I also need to organize my "YOU! the Brand." materials so I can keep moving forward toward my BGP goals. I welcome travel days because they force me to substitute the comfort and routine of my office for the discomfort and chaos of airports, airplanes, and hotels. I love the change of pace and place. It changes my perspective, which always adds a new dimension to my projects.

Summarize your goal: By 12/31/06 "YOU! the Brand." will have 1,000 subscribers generating gross revenues of $35,000 a month. By 4/15/06 "YOU! the Brand." will have 10 subscribers generating gross revenues of $350 a month. And, by 4/22/06 "YOU! the Brand." will commit to at least 100 "YOU! the Brand." installations with each generating at least $4,000 a month.

How will you know when you reach your goal? The proceeds from the credit card, ACH, and check transactions will be in eSMART Communications bank account.

What would you like to accomplish during the 2 week program? Adopt a sustainable thought and action pattern that breaks big goals into bite-size chunks and helps me ask for assistance from others when I encounter obstacles.

Daily Practice—List what you did (shares, actions, requests):

My new elevator speech (with credit and thanks to Lisa) goes like this: "'YOU! The Brand.' makes it easy for you to establish a professional looking travel blog that will help build your business. You can add personal posts whenever you like, but we keep your blog fresh and up-to-date by posting up to 4 interesting travel-related items for you every week. You choose the look-and-feel of your blog, but we take care of a lot of the work for you. All this and more costs less than $2 a day." I shared this new elevator speech and my goals with Cindy XXXXX from XXXXX and Bob and Debbie XXXXX from XXXXX. Their comments and enthusiasm for the service created my first BKE (see BKE section below for more details). Additionally, I asked them to review an e-mail that I will send on Monday that will contain a draft of the new promotional "story" that Lisa drafted after Saturday's one-on-one conference call. I created a special interest group in ACT! for "YOU! the Brand." advisors and added 84 individuals to the group. The new promotional copy will be sent to the entire group with a request for suggestions and edits. The BGPs are part of this group. I also wrote and sent a "backdrop" piece to the BGPs explaining the transition from travel agents (compensated by suppliers) to travel advocates (compensated by consumers).

List any other actions: I consumed too much wine at dinner.

List any results: I felt good about the number of tasks I completed today and found it more comfortable to share and ask.

List any breakthroughs you experienced today (not expected every day, but you never know!): My biggest obstacle has been explaining the features, advantages, and benefits of "YOU! the Brand." Lisa helped me focus on the blogging portion of the "YOU! the Brand." bundle of services. She also crafted a story about "YOU! the Brand." that eliminated my obstacle. The "deer-in-headlights" looks that I've received during the past few weeks, were suddenly replaced with "ah-ha!" looks as I recited my new "YOU! the Brand." elevator speech to Cindy, Bob, and Debbie. This BKE was cause for celebration which led to my consumption of too much wine! Oh well! If that's the price of a BKE, bring 'em on!

Any other comments: I am really excited about Day 2's theme— Conversations for the Change. I'm in the right place (FLL) at the right time (presenting a workshop at a Cruise-sellers conference) to maximize the outcome of those conversations.

## Day 2—Monday

How are you feeling today?

Other than the aftereffects of yesterday evening's self-inflicted wine overindulgence, I feel great. I'm excited to practice my new "YOU! the Brand." elevator speech, ask my new group of advisors for feedback about my e-promotion, and to present my workshop at the Cruise 360 conference.

Daily Practice—List what you did (shares, actions, requests): I gave my elevator speech and shared my goals to Jim XXXXX of XXXXX and to Aimee XXXXX of XXXXX. I sent a copy of my e-promotion to my group of 88 advisors (including the BGP group) and asked for their feedback and suggestions. I acknowledged feedback from several of the early responders.

List any other actions: I edited my workshop content to position "YOU! the Brand." as a solution to "Fighting Discounting & Rebating by Selling Yourself First." I also reconnected the DNS for www.you-the-brand.com web site and validated that it is now linking correctly.

List any results: I received four bounced emails from my list of advisors. Tomorrow, I will ask Chantalle to track down the correct e-mail addresses so I can re-send those "Advisors" my e-promotion for their feedback

List any breakthroughs you experienced today (not expected every day, but you never know!): Peggy XXXXX and Managing Editor of XXXXX magazine responded to my request for feedback, gave me several good edits, and asked if I would set up a complimentary "YOU! the Brand." system for her so she could write about it firsthand. Of course, I agreed and immediately reserved XXXXX and will have her blog and e-mail account activated on Tuesday. Having a respected trade press editor write about "YOU! the Brand." from firsthand experience is the best and least expensive form of advertising I could buy.

My second BKE came from Sandi XXXXX and Vice President of XXXXX. She is part of my advisory group and agreed to promote "YOU! the Brand." to each of regional XXXXX. XXXXX has more than 1,000 professional leisure travel sellers who would benefit from "YOU! the Brand."

Any other comments: I can't wait to begin Day 3 and return to Chicago!

## Day 3—Tuesday

How are you feeling today? Energized. Up at 4:30a ET to catch a flight to Chicago. In my office by 1:00p CT for a conference call. And, at 4:30p to the off-leash dog park for some exercise for the dogs and me. I've watched my diet during this trip (with the exception of Sunday night's Bacchus bash) and that has really help keep my mental and physical energy high.

Daily Practice—List what you did (shares, actions, requests): I shared my goal with Rose XXXXX, our company attorney, and with Kate XXXXX, our PR consultant

List any other actions: Submitted 1700 word "Attacking Discounting & Rebating" article to XXXXX. The article positions "YOU! the Brand." as one solution for attacking discounting and rebating. Responded to 33 replies to my request for feedback and incorporated advisors' suggestions in promotional copy.

List any results: Article was accepted for publication in April 2006 issue of Home Based Trade

List any breakthroughs you experienced today (not expected every day, but you never know!): Had a great experience onboard AA1241 from MIA to ORD—Recorded in my Blog (www.ahlsmith.com)

Any other comments: There's no place like home!

## Day 4—Wednesday

How are you feeling today?

Fabulous! Great energy. Clear focus. Positive outlook. Drugs in the 70s weren't this good!

Daily Practice—List what you did (shares, actions, requests): Shared my goals with Diane XXXXX, meeting planner, and Brian XXXXX, CFO of XXXXX

Sent request for coffee or lunch with Andy XXXXX, author of Blog Wild!, plus requests for phone feedback from Shel XXXXX, co-author of XXXXX, and Jeremy XXXXX, author of XXXXX.

Edited my elevator speech using edits suggested by several advisors, and after asking Lisa, I postponed the email broadcast originally scheduled for tomorrow so as not to compete with Passover and Easter plans. This also gives me time to work on an order entry process . . . forgot about that!

List any results: Received an offer from Joel XXXXX, editor and publisher of XXXXX to create and run banner ads and podcasts for "YOU! the Brand." on XXXXX in exchange podcasts promoting his two annual cruise conferences.

Diane XXXXX, editor of XXXXX magazine asked me to write a technology (think blogs and brands!) article for the June issue. Received a reply from Shel XXXXX saying he was too busy for a phone call, but offered to answer my questions through email. I'll take it! Advice from Shel? Priceless!

List any breakthroughs you experienced today (not expected every day, but you never know!): Received a call from XXXXX, founder and former COO of XXXXX and now launching two new luxury XXXXX brands: XXXXX. He is one of my 89 advisors. He called to suggest two changes to my e-promotion copy. Then he said that he'd instructed his VP of Sales and Marketing to work with me to have at least 100 custom "YOU! the Brand." sites linked to top professional travel sellers during June. He wants the Blog contest to talk about luxury hotel experiences. It just doesn't get much better, because he is branding guru (think Lexus!) and whatever he endorses is sought after by the rest of the industry.

Any other comments:

Sam, Bucca, and I had a great romp at the off-leash dog park this evening. I feel that Lisa's BKE system is taking me off-leash!

## Day 5—Thursday

How are you feeling today?

Thank goodness for Advil and a Positive Mental Attitude! My back is out of alignment, but it only hurts when I breathe!

Daily Practice—List what you did (shares, actions, requests):

Shares: Bob XXXXX (see Requests) and Barry XXXXX, home-based travel professional and podcaster

Actions: Had a conference call with the VP of National Accounts and the National Sales Manager for XXXXX and got their commitment to accept my proposal for 500 "YOU! the Brand." subscriptions that would give XXXXX access to more than 100,000 households (200 per travel seller) at least four times per week. This works out to less than 18 cents per month per household. They will receive my proposal on Monday.

Requests: Added Bob XXXXX, Travel Industry Marketing Executive for XXXXX, to my Advisors Group and requested his feedback on the promotional message for next Tuesday's broadcast.

List any other actions: Created a process flow for order entry and billing.

List any results: Got some new story ideas from Seth Godin's Blog and links to other copywriters' blogs.

List any breakthroughs you experienced today (not expected every day, but you never know!): Nothing today, which helped me catch-up and capitalize on the week's progress.

Any other comments: I'm excited to learn more about Joshua's goals in tomorrow's one-on-one.

### Day 6—Friday

How are you feeling today?

My back is still out of whack, but a few good stretches and a boxcar-size dosage of Advil are helping my back catch-up with my mind.

Daily Practice—List what you did (shares, actions, requests):

Today was appropriately named. My first what-if occurred yesterday when I received an order. Today I focused order processing, accounting, user agreements, and the mechanics of establishing a domain name, setting-up an email account, and creating a blog. I'm not good at details and I really have to force myself to stay focused. I also know from past experience that I cannot manage what I cannot do. So, before I could off-load all the order entry details to Chantalle, Pam, and Robin, I needed to do them myself.

List any other actions: I should know this by now, but I can go for days without "accomplishing" anything because I'm not "doing" anything. Then as soon as I start "doing" something other things start to appear. It's like "inactivity begets more inactivity" and "action begets action." As I said, this shouldn't be a revelation. It happens over and over again.

Anyway, now that I'm up to my neck in "YOU! the Brand." and I'm "sharing" and "requesting" and "acting," I receive a phone call from Moscow—not Idaho, but the one in Russia. A large holding company purchased the State-owned travel, tour, and hotel company, XXXXX and is planning rapid expansion. They need a travel technology platform that integrates reservations, inventory control, yield management, CRM, customer loyalty administration, and much more.

I was recommended for the job and all I had to do was prepare a presentation and deliver it during a teleconference 9:00a Tuesday morning, Moscow time. That would be midnight Monday in Chicago.

This is one of those "dream" assignments. One that I've spent 35 years preparing for. And, one that has two commas in the paycheck. Like appearing on The O'Reilly Factor and testifying before a Congressional Sub-committee, I feel frightened and anxious, but I had to agree to do it. I don't know how I'm going to pull this off. I also don't know how I can keep "YOU! the Brand." moving forward at the same time.

Lots to think about tonight so I'm taking the dogs to the off-leash park. My back can't get any worse and a 90 minute walk combined with happy dogs always helps me sort things out.

List any breakthroughs you experienced today (not expected every day, but you never know!): Probably some here somewhere, but I'm too scattered to identify them.

Any other comments: The "what-if" exercise produced the following:

What if "YOU! the Brand." tasted like dark chocolate?

What if "YOU! the Brand." had 50K subscribers—half the potential market?

What if "YOU! the Brand." became a story rather than a bundle of services?

What if "YOU! the Brand." became as well known as Carnival Cruise Lines?

What if "YOU! the Brand." had 25 ruthless competitors?

What if "YOU! the Brand." put all its competitors out of business?

What if "YOU! the Brand." changed its name to "YOU! the Blog."?

What if "YOU! the Brand." liked to listen to classical music?

What if "YOU! the Brand." preferred rap?

What if "YOU! the Brand." tasted like a Grand Mariner soufflé?

What if "YOU! the Brand." changed its name to "YOU! the Glob."?

What if "YOU! the Brand." became popular with hair stylists?

What if "YOU! the Brand." was a 50-something DWF?

What if "YOU! the Brand." loved dogs?

What if "YOU! the Brand." was acquired for $18 million?

## Day 7–Saturday

How are you feeling today?

Took an extra hour getting-up this morning. Enjoyed coffee-in-bed. And looked at the chaos I created from a horizontal rather than a vertical perspective. That helped. Also, I didn't notice until about 3p that my back was fine. No Advil today!

Daily Practice—List what you did (shares, actions, requests): Joshua and I had very productive one-on-one. I like his "hub" consumer network and enjoyed talking through the in-person feedback calls he planned to make early next week. Joshua help me enormously by suggesting that on Monday I create a mythical, but urgent, order or two for "YOU! the Brand." He also suggested that I step aside and watch how Chantalle, Pam and Robin handle the order and the pressure. This "trial run" will help validate the order processing flow I created yesterday.

List any other actions: Analysis is a perfect theme for today. I really need to listen to the data, weigh my options, and alter my course to achieve my "YOU! the Brand." goals and win the Moscow contract.

List any results: Lisa's Breakthrough coaching, even though I'm only half way through the 14 days, gave me the confidence to continue accomplishing my "YOU! the Brand." goals while establishing an additional goal of winning the Moscow consulting contract. I know I can accomplish both goals.

A term Lisa introduced in one of her blog postings, "chunking", gives me this confidence. As I understand the term, "chunking" it involves dedicating "chunks" of time to different activities, but ensuring that each chunk of dedicated time moves the project forward in a meaningful way. "Chunking" is an antidote for "multi-tasking" which creates a flurry of short activities without a requirement for any activity to accomplish something before moving to the next. "Multi-tasking" creates commotion while "chunking" creates results.

List any breakthroughs you experienced today (not expected every day, but you never know!): BKE Chunking.

## Day 8—Sunday

How are you feeling today?

Calm. Thoughtful. Reverent. Confident.

Daily Practice—List what you did (shares, actions, requests): My "wild idea" is that I can write a proposal that will win a multimillion Euro consulting contract and deliver that proposal by telephone tomorrow night to an audience in Moscow that will be evaluating my proposal through an interpreter. At the same time, I will find a "chunk" of time to take all the feedback I received from my group of advisors to rewrite the "YOU! the Brand." broadcast to 20K prospects on Tuesday. I will also find another "chunk" of time to implement Joshua's suggestion to organize an "urgent order" fire drill for my "YOU! the Brand." staff on Monday.

## Day 9—Monday

How are you feeling today? Nervous and apprehensive. I've got a lot on my plate and I'm feeling apprehensive

Daily Practice—List what you did (shares, actions, requests): I made five "YOU! the Brand." requests by telephone and five by e-mail. Two of my telephone requests were to individuals who were initially critical when they first heard of "YOU! the Brand." I requested their ideas to transform "YOU! the Brand." into a service they could support. I sense I caught them off guard!

List any other actions: I gave Chantalle, Pam, and Robin two mythical, but "rush" orders. They didn't know the orders were not real. They did a very good job and filled the orders in less than four hours. They discovered several gaps in the process flow I created last week, so as Joshua suggested, the "fire drill" paid big dividends.

Most importantly it gave me one less item on my plate as I finished my Moscow consulting proposal.

List any results: In order to "chunk" I needed to turn off my phone and e-mail. Both of those distracted me from accomplishing what I had required from each "chunk" of time. I really learned how ineffective "multi-tasking" can be.

### Day 10–Tuesday

Daily Practice—I embraced time chunking again today. It really boosts my productivity. When my mind wanders, I make a note in a "parking lot" journal I carry with me. It's a good way to record the random thought and immediately return to my focus on the current chunk of time.

List any other actions: I made a list of 10 suppliers that I will blitz tomorrow and pitch them on sponsoring 100 or more "YOU! the Brand." blogs. The suppliers are: XXXXX, XXXXX, and XXXXX

List any results: I received more feedback from the Magellan office staff regarding process and work flow regarding orders.

Any other comments: I am more excited about my goal than ever. Getting more than 1,000 travel professionals paying an average of $35 a month for "YOU! the Brand." subscriptions is clear and achievable. The only addition I am making is that I'm focusing on depositing $35,000 a month in eSMART Communications checking account. That motivates me more than selling 1,000 subscriptions @ $35

### Day 11–Wednesday

Daily Practice—Today is a travel day. I arrived in Boston about 10am and had meetings at The Travel Institute throughout the afternoon. I made four calls while driving from Logan Airport to Wellesley, MA and received encouragement from all four for my 20,000 households impressions per week concept. Throughout the afternoon I completed four more calls with equally good reception.

Although I did not complete all 10 calls during my action blitz, I completed 8 and kept up with my commitments to The Travel Institute.

List any breakthroughs you experienced today (not expected every day, but you never know!): Multitasking while driving is OK as long as the first priority is driving, otherwise chunking is much more productive. I completed four preliminary sales calls while driving from Logan to Wellesley. That normally would have been unproductive time.

### Day 12–Thursday

How are you feeling today? Partly cloudy. I stayed out too late last night enjoying Boston's North End. My 5:00 a.m. wake-up call this morning came far too early, but I suited-up and was on the court in time for the game.

Daily Practice—List what you did (shares, actions, requests): I shared my goal with The Travel Institute's staff and requested their support. I answered more than 40 e-mails generated by Wednesday's e-broadcast.

List any other actions: I organized my responses to the e-mails inquiring about "YOU! the Brand." so I can add them to the FAQ on www.you-the-brand.com. Wrote two e-mails following-up on questions regarding the Moscow consulting opportunity.

List any results: Received 6 "YOU! the Brand." subscription orders @ $39.95/month.

Received an invitation to speak at Luxury Travel Expo in Las Vegas in December. This is the largest U.S. travel show of the year, so the exposure is awesome.

List any breakthroughs you experienced today (not expected every day, but you never know!): Now that I'm well into the second half of my fifties, I've realized that I can't party like I did during the second half of my twenties. I know that probably doesn't sound like a breakthrough, but I had to push the envelope to learn for myself.

Any other comments: None that won't incriminate me!

I volunteer at least two days each month as Chairman of The Travel Institute (www.thetravelinstitute.com), a 42 year-old not-for-profit organization that provides continuing education, designations, and academic certifications for travel professionals. Today was my second day of a 2-day visit to The Travel Institute's Wellesley, MA headquarters. Today's theme prompted me to reassess my role at The Travel Institute, my motives, and the outcomes.

After this assessment, I understood why I volunteered my time (to give back to an industry that has given me so much), how I could make a difference (sharing my BKEs from Lisa's 14-day program with the Wellesley staff), and how might I help the staff achieve BKEs (shares, actions, requests).

Today's results were outstanding. The staff overcame three roadblocks that had stalled three major revenue-generating initiatives. One of the roadblocks fell prey to setting-up a Google Group to facilitate discussions without the need for a standing conference call. Another solution came from a request for feedback made by the organization's marketing manager to obtain some new software to help her track her e-marketing responses. The third outcome resolved a financial issue that kept us from moving forward with an international contract for training and certification in Dubai. This outcome materialized because our sales manager shared our challenge with one of our largest customers who has international contacts. The customer agreed to have their international attorneys review our licensing agreement pro bono.

I love being on the court and in the game, but today I loved being on the sidelines and coaching a dedicated group toward completion of their goals. I'll remember this day for a long time. It really proves the adage, "the more you give, the more you get."

Today also showed the value of "chunking." I reserved "chunks" of time with specific and measurable outcomes for The Travel Institute, "YOU! the Brand.", the Moscow consulting project, and Magellan Travel Group. During each reserved "chunk" of time I only focused on tasks and conversations that moved me closer to that "chunks" outcome. I turned-off my phone, e-mail, and IM and concentrated on the people responsible for each task. At the end of the day I was amazed by the progress in all four areas.

### Day 13—Friday

How are you feeling today? Positive and confident.

Daily Practice—List what you did (shares, actions, requests). I shared my goal with Doug XXXXX of XXXXX and asked for his thoughts about bundling his new product (XXXXX) with "YOU! the Brand." His product will enter beta testing next week and he thought a bundle of "YOU! the Brand." and XXXXX would benefit both products. I secured appointments in NYC next Tuesday and Wednesday with Sue XXXXX (travel industry consultant), Martin XXXXX (travel trade show promoter), Joanne XXXXX (travel press), Debbie XXXXX (e-marketing specialist) and Ann XXXXX (graphic artist). Each of these individuals will be able to support a different aspect of "YOU! the Brand."

List any other actions: Traveled from Boston to Chicago.

List any results: Received three more "YOU! the Brand" subscriptions @ $39.95/month.

Any other comments: Usually, I've devoted travel days to reflection and introspection. Today, my mind kept racing forward. My To-Do List grows, but I have it segmented into "chunks" that correspond with my goals. This system gives me a "parking lot" for thoughts and ideas from other "chunks" that would have previously interrupted the "chunk" that was presently in focus. Of course, in the past I rationalized those interruptions and labeled them "multi-tasking!"

You have had some time to explore and play around with your goal, but are you being it? Yes. Definitely, yes. When I awoke this morning and headed for Logan Airport, I WAS the owner of "YOU! the Brand." and was thinking about how to secure our 2nd thousand subscriptions. I could feel and see the future and it was exactly how I had hoped it would be.

If your goal is to build a successful business—are you thinking and acting like a successful business person?

Yes. I noticed a number of people nodding, smiling, and saying, "Good morning!" as we passed in the airport concourse this morning. This is the aura of success.

## Day 14—Saturday

How are you feeling today? Positive and confident.

Daily Practice—List what you did (shares, actions, requests). I shared my goal with Ray XXXXX, President of XXXXX and asked for his thoughts about sponsoring 100 "YOU! the Brand." blogs for his top sales producers. I showed him how XXXXX could reach 20,000 households every week for less than 20 cents per household per week. I asked Ray to share my proposal with his VP of Marketing and Sales to get their input.

List any other actions: Drafted three sales inquiry follow-up letters to be sent to prospective subscribers.

Any other comments: Today is bittersweet in that it combines the ending of an outstanding 14-day coaching session and begins a new and exciting era. I feel like the baby bird that is being pushed from the nest. Excited and scared.

Please provide me feedback about the program!

1. Did you experience any breakthroughs?

Oh, let me count the ways! One thing I learned is that breakthroughs come in all shapes and sizes. I also learned that small breakthroughs grow larger as their piece of the puzzle is more clearly defined. The moral of this is to never discount a breakthrough, no matter how large or small.

2. Did you enjoy the program?

Yes. It was clarifying, enlightening, and motivating. I broke several bad habits and installed several new good habits.

3. What were your favorite, least favorite parts of the program?

I enjoyed the entire program. The most difficult tasks for me were the "requests." Men weren't wired to ask for directions or for assistance, but I forced myself to get over it and the results were phenomenal.

4. What recommendations do you have for improving the program?

Make one of the one-on-ones a peer-to-peer exercise. We all benefited from interviewing and coaching each other.

5. Would you recommend the program to others?

Absolutely. If your goal was to create raving fans, you succeeded!

6. What advice would you give people who pick up the book and are getting ready to begin the program?

Make sure your goal is yours and not one that you or someone else thinks you should achieve. To make this program work, you really have to believe in your goal. You need the type of passion for your goal that wakes you up before the alarm, motivates you to complete your shares, requests, and actions before 10am, and occupies every creative thought while in the shower. When you add your breakthrough technologies to this kind of passion, the magic starts to happen and the results are astounding.

Thank you. Thank you. Thank you.

My follow-up question to Scott, one month after the program ended.

*The program ended one month ago. How have you been doing relative to your goal in the last month? Are you still using the techniques from the program?*

I'm still tracking to exceed my year-end goal. I've had some unexpected setbacks and some surprise breakthroughs. The daily routine of Lisa's Breakthrough Program tends to even out the highs and the lows and that helps me stay focused on the outcome.

One of the more interesting aspects of this program is how easily the "share, request, and action" activities integrated into my daily routine. "Share, request, action" quickly became a mantra that lurks in my subconscious and bubbles to the surface when appropriate. When I feel discouraged, I request some feedback or share my goal with the first person I encounter. Wanting to get back on the horse that bucked me off is a great confidence booster.

I've set up recurring daily activities in my calendar program for the next five years. At 7:00 A.M. I'm reminded to share my goal with two people. At 7:15 A.M. Lisa reminds me to make two requests for help or feedback relating to my goal. And, at 7:30 A.M. I take two actions toward completing my goal. As Lisa's Breakthrough Program prescribes, I complete this routine every day, seven days a week. It's become as routine as my daily vitamins and morning cups of coffee.

This daily routine also helps remind me about the benefits of "chunking"—dedicating "chunks" of time to a single activity rather than multitasking and paying partial attention to several activities all happening at once. Starting each day by completing at least six goal-oriented activities before 8:00 A.M. gets each day off to a great start and ignites a chain of breakthrough experiences.

# References

## Books

Lee, G. *Courage: The Backbone of Leadership*. San Francisco: Jossey-Bass, 2006.

Perkins, D. *Archimedes' Bathtub*. New York: Norton, 2000.

Schwartz, D. *The Magic of Thinking Big*. New York: Fireside, 1987.

von Oech, R. *A Whack on the Side of the Head*. New York: Warner Books, 1998.

Zander, R. S., and Zander, B. *The Art of Possibility: Transforming Personal and Professional Life*. New York: Penguin, 2000.

## Weblogs and Web Sites

Gratzon, F. "For My Next Trick," May 13, 2005. *The Lazy Way to Success*, http://lazyway.blogs.com/lazy_way/2005/05/for_my_next_tri.html. Access date: July 10, 2006.

JKF Moon Speech—Rice Stadium, September 12, 1962. NASA, http://www1.jsc.nasa.gov/er/seh/ricetalk.htm. Access date: July 10, 2006.

Richards, D. "Ask for What You Want," May 21, 2005. *Come Gather Round*, www.ongenius.com/blog/index.php/2005/05/21/asking-for-what-you-want/. Access date: July 10, 2006.

# The Author

*Lisa Haneberg* is an expert in the areas of management, leadership, and personal and organizational success. She consults in the areas of organization development, management and leadership training, and human resources. Haneberg also offers integrated training solutions and individual and group coaching services. She is an enthusiastic and enjoyable presenter and speaker available to address a variety of leadership and management topics.

Her first book, *High Impact Middle Management: Solutions for Today's Busy Managers*, broke new ground for its audience (Adams Media, 2005). She has also written *Focus Like a Laser Beam: Ten Ways to Do What Matters Most* (Jossey-Bass, 2006), *Organization Development Basics* (ASTD, 2005), and *Coaching Basics* (ASTD, 2006). Lisa reaches a worldwide audience through her popular management blog called Management Craft (www.managementcraft.com and www.allbusiness.com). Management Craft offers resources and perspectives to leaders, managers, and those who develop and coach them. Her main Web site, www.lisahaneberg.com, highlights her products and services.

Over the past twenty-two years, Lisa has worked with leaders at all levels and for many types and sizes of organizations—high tech-manufacturing (Intel); distribution, manufacturing, and services (Black & Decker, Mead Paper, Corbis); e-retailing and distribution (Amazon.com); travel and leisure products and services (Beacon Hotel, Travcoa, and Cruise West); and the Royal Government of Thailand. She is a certified master trainer and behavioral assessment interpreter. She earned an undergraduate degree in Behavioral

Sciences from the University of Maryland and has taken graduate courses at Johns Hopkins University, Ohio State University, and Goddard College.

Lisa Haneberg lives in the beautiful Pacific Northwest with her husband, four dogs, and two cats. She enjoys travel, reading, writing, and driving her motorcycle down winding roads.

# Index